# The Adaptive Conversation Process

## A Leader's Guide to More Effective Conversations in an Ever-Changing World

**Nicholas Phillips**

**Suri Surinder**

# In partnership with CTR Factor

3848 Flatiron Loop, Suite 102, Tampa, FL 33544

**For information regarding speaking engagements or for programming to bring the Adaptive Conversation Process to your company, contact:**

Email: info@CTRfactor.com

Web: CTRfactor.com

Phone: 1 (877) 275-9472

ISBN: 9798312701258

First Printing: 2025

# CONTENTS

SECTION THREE

# THE ADAPTIVE CONVERSATION PROCESS: A MODEL IN PRACTICE

==========================================

SECTION FOUR

# THE ADAPTIVE CONVERSATION PROCESS: TOOLBOX

==========================================

I

# INTRODUCTION

Why do leaders sometimes avoid having important conversations, and when they do, why are some of those conversations simply…less effective than they could be? Is it a lack of confidence in knowing how to approach the many different types of conversations they have? Is it fear of conflict or consequence if the conversation gets off track? Is it just too difficult - too confusing amid so many frameworks - or does it simply take too much effort to get it right? The reality is, all of these are reasons why leaders avoid, or can be less effective, in their conversations, and in an ever-changing world there is more urgency now than ever before.

Leaders have so many conversations with their team members every day. If they are to get the most out of those conversations they must reflect and plan, so wouldn't all leaders appreciate a way to make things easier? **Wouldn't it be great if we could be more efficient in preparing for conversational effectiveness?**

We all have models, processes, and frameworks that we have studied and tried throughout our time as leaders. We tend to use what works for us, and there is value in most models out there. Yet, there is a fundamental truth that still exists. Before going into a conversation, we must take time to pause and think about all those models sitting in the wings, and only once we know "which type" of conversation we are about to have can we then choose the model or process or framework that we will follow. I don't know about you, but that reality sounds exhausting.

Wouldn't it be great - wouldn't it be a little less exhausting - if before each conversation rather than having to decide which among the many to pull forward based on the conversation at hand, instead **we could have in our pocket a single process model that could be easily adapted broadly**?

It can get both confusing and time consuming when you need to pause and figure out which type of conversation you are about to have…and then ponder, compare, decide, recall, and finally select the one you might follow for that specific type of conversation. It is for this reason that the conversation process model we have developed is so unique and effective. **Its greatest strength comes from the fact that it is adaptive, meaning the simple step-by-step process can be used effectively, and consistently, being adapted for different types of conversations.** It allows you to be present in the conversation, actively listen to the other person, and have an anchor to refer to by simply asking yourself, "at what step in the process is our conversation currently?"

While the conversation process model we have developed provides a single progression for effective conversations, it does not require that you forego your pre-existing philosophical frameworks, whose tenets you may have adhered to over time. It is not just a theoretical model. It reflects the practical conversation techniques we have used throughout our careers as consultants, team leaders, executives, and colleagues to lead organizations, foster inclusion, and drive change.

**Every single leader we shared this with agreed and wished it was something they "had last week,"** obviously thinking of a coaching or mentoring session, or a performance conversation, or a teaching opportunity they recently had with someone on their team.

Our book is a deep dive into this conversation process model, and the workshop we bring to companies teaches leaders how to have effective conversations using this process – whether coaching, mentoring, performance, consulting, advising, teaching, training, change, etc.

# PREFACE

# Birth of the
# Adaptive Conversation Process

## SOMETIMES THERE'S MORE THAN ONE WAY

I remember back in middle and high school, my father impressed upon me the importance of mathematics. He was an electrician by trade, so you might expect that was the reason for him placing such an importance on the subject. If I brought home my report card with Bs (or even the occasional C) in Social Studies, or Science, or pretty much anything other than math it was just fine...but anything less than an A in math seemed to be the end of the world in his eyes.

He'd often sit down and watch as I did my homework. I could feel his excitement over my shoulder when I'd have an algebra problem that required a full-page worth of "showing my work." What I always found interesting was that occasionally he would show me a different way to solve a problem, adapting use of other mathematical concepts to get to the same answer.

He'd tell me, *"Not always, but sometimes, you can use one thing and apply it in different ways to suit varying conditions. Sometimes, there's more than one way."*

Of course, at the time, I was learning the most followed process, one which was supposedly the most correct way in the eyes of the masses. We were, as it seemed, simply expected to "do as it's always been." I just wanted to get my homework done and had to solve the way our teacher was showing us, but he just could not help himself. He would tell me that I "could" use the technique being taught...but I could also get to the correct answer a different way. He was my dad, and the answer he would get was always correct, so there was no sense in arguing. I'd just say thanks and move on to the next question, but in class the next day I could rarely help myself from "teaching my teacher" if there was another way. Usually, the response was something to the effect of, *"yes you are right, but everyone follows this process and we're learning it this way right now."*

I could usually tell, however, that the teacher appreciated my out-of-the box thinking. I knew early on that sometimes there's simply more than one way.

## LEADERS CAN CHOOSE TO DO THINGS DIFFERENTLY

I remember when I was a young professional. I was working in my very first management role for a high-end residential home builder based in Atlanta Georgia. My responsibilities were managing our receptionists, couriers, mail room, and office machines & supplies. I had never directly led others before, so I had no immediate experiences to pull from and everything in front of me to learn (...more than twenty-some-odd years later, I'm still learning).

I formed relationships with as many managers as I could, and I made it a point to engage in conversations with directors, vice presidents, and even our chairman of the board whenever the opportunity arose. I became a sponge and tried to soak up as much knowledge and experience as they could spill my way because, well...I had to play the part where I was at while I learned how to do it well and get where I needed to be. Some of what I learned seemed pretty straightforward, but providing feedback and especially having conversations around things like coaching, advising, and performance seemed to be something everyone had a different approach to. If it was already widely adopted, they just assumed that was the best way to do things, or if it was something they already applied it was just easier to stick with what was already in place.

My boss at the time (he was in the U.S. Navy Reserve) had a military type of approach in most conversation he had as a leader. "Briefly state the issue...Be factual in your statements...Be direct and then dismiss." Good bad or otherwise, this was the approach he told me to follow.

Our director of design had a positive-first approach to different leader conversations. "Be upbeat and express something encouraging...Address performance (or whatever was being discussed) with opportunity in mind...Be supportive in helping to create a way forward." It aligned well with her overall personality.

Our chief information technology officer followed a logic-first technique: Talk about results...acknowledge logical root causes...discuss rationale around change & consequence...agree on hypotheses." I'm not trying to generalize, but the process he followed and the way he would deliver it across different types of conversations came across like he was writing code, but with people.

Of course, I've paraphrased these slightly but believe me these were some of the conversation processes followed by those very experienced professionals. I respected them, but something inside me knew they couldn't aways work, in every situation, and I needed something better. I found myself preparing for one of my very first formal conversations with one of my team members, so I walked upstairs to "executive row" and asked the Chief Human Resources Officer which one was "best."

He told me that there was "value" in them all, and leaders can choose to do things differently.

Well, that was helpful. NOT! I think he just wanted me to spend time contemplating what technique would work well for me as opposed to giving me "his preferred approach," and he didn't want to disparage the tactics of those other leaders. It left me, however, still wondering which one to choose for myself, and for the kind of conversation I was preparing for. I can't even remember exactly what I did...but I think I used a little from each and crossed my fingers hoping I did a halfway decent job.


## ALRIGHT...THEY'RE ALL RIGHT

Fast forward many years and several organizations later. After a handful of leadership roles, a lot of learning, openness to new ways and ideas, and broad leadership exposure while running a consulting firm, I found myself working for an established company in a capacity where I could build their leadership and organizational development department from the ground up. From leadership training at all levels, to behavioral 360-assessments, to probing into challenges of individual and team effectiveness, to deliberate interpersonal discussions and more, I found myself researching, reflecting, and executing through so many different models and frameworks used across the board. There was so much to choose from.

I started getting really interested in coaching, from first-time managers all the way up to senior executives. I studied best practices through reading and engaging in conversations with leaders at my company and across my network. I engaged with an executive coach myself, who was very experienced as a seasoned leadership development coach and who doubled as the team psychiatrist for a Super Bowl champion football team. I read books and attended programs including formal education in multiple world-renowned coaching disciplines...and yet, what I found time and again were simply more questions.

There seemed to be many complementary models at play across the board, which spanned everything from the use of intentional positive phraseology, to compassionate inquiry, to concepts of individual change and more. There were some that focused on stages people go through. There were others that concentrated on the specifics of word choice and how to have a specific type of meeting dialogue. There were those that drew distinct lines between types of conversations, and there were even those that prescribed when two-way dialogue was part of the approach and when it was not.

Amid innumerable models, processes, frameworks, and opinions coming from well-respected sources in the world to choose from, the question of which was best still haunted me even though I knew that there was value in them all.

I still wondered: Which one is best? Which one works? Which one should I choose, and for which situation or conversation?

Excited and confused all at the same time I came to realize something which, on the surface, may seem obvious though for some reason it still felt like a light bulb going off in my head.

I think I even said it out loud when I told myself, "They're all right."

Each approach, every technique, all the models - they were crafted by smart people and delivered by capable and experienced professionals. They were applied by countless leaders, have value, and work. So why did choosing "the best one" still seem so difficult?

And then, that light bulb grew brighter...and an idea was born.

## SO MANY OPTIONS...SO LITTLE TIME

I stepped into my first people-leader role (by title) on February 8, 1999. That was a long time ago, and it illustrates how many years since I have been exposed to so many different models and approaches to having conversations with diverse individuals on my team. From those leaders who shared with me back in my early days, to the research and studying I've done over time and in recent years, I came to realize something important. Although there is certainly value in all those countless models being used by leaders today, and while there are certainly those that come to mind more readily than others, there is still a fundamental requisite question leaders must ask before "choosing" which to use. That question is: "What kind of conversation am I about to have?"

And, if that question must first be answered, then it stands to reason that it takes time and effort to then refer to a litany of models just waiting in the wings to be accessed when called upon and decide which makes most sense based on the conversation to be had. I thought, "great...another step in trying to determine 'the best' one to apply." Until it hit me.

Leaders have so many conversations with their team members every day. If they are to get the most out of those conversations they must reflect and plan, so wouldn't all leaders appreciate a way to make things easier? Wouldn't it be great if we could be more efficient in preparing for conversational effectiveness?

When I spoke with leaders about how they prepare to coach, they seemed to know going in which coaching approach, among many, they may follow.

When those leaders had to sit down for a change conversation with a team member, they almost always considered in advance which change process would influence their dialogue.

When they found it necessary to have a difficult performance conversation with an individual, they certainly pre-planned the conversation by deciding which process was best and how they would engage intentionally.

I am no different than any of these leaders. I am no different from you or anyone reading this book. We all have models, processes, and frameworks that we've studied and tried throughout our time as leaders. We tend to use what works for us, and there is value in most models out there. Yet, there is a fundamental truth that still exists. Before going into a conversation, we must take time to pause and think about all those models sitting in the wings, and only once we know "which type" of conversation we are about to have can we then choose the model or process or framework that we'll follow. I don't know about you, but that reality sounds exhausting.

And then...it became clear.

## ONE PROCESS

I don't mean to sound pretentious. I have absolute respect for many of the different models that exist, and I follow many tenets of them myself. But wouldn't it be great - wouldn't it be a little less exhausting - if before each conversation rather than having to decide which among the many to pull forward based on the conversation at hand, instead we could have in our pocket a single process model that could be easily adapted broadly?

Wouldn't it be great if we had one single process to follow for so many of the conversations that we leaders have? The value from all those varied models developed by some of the smartest people over centuries could still influence leadership style and philosophy, guiding how you approach leadership and engaging in valuable dialogue with your folks, but your pre-planning and the conversation itself could become so much easier.

It was so obvious to me. Every single leader I shared this with agreed and wished it was something they "had last week," obviously thinking of a coaching or mentoring session or a performance conversation or a teaching opportunity they recently had with someone on their team.

And so...the Adaptive Conversation Process was born.

# SECTION ONE

## THE ADAPTIVE CONVERSATION PROCESS:

### *ONE PROCESS*

# 1.0

# Power in a Single Process Model

## POWER TO ADAPT

Certainly, a lot has been published on topics of general communication, coaching dialogue, mentoring discourse, performance discussions, consulting conversations, and more. As a leader, it can sometimes get a bit overwhelming, trying approach after approach...process after process...model after model to see what works for you.

In collaborating and sharing with countless leaders, we often hear that they pick a tactic and practice it for a while, finding that it works well with a certain type of conversation but not so much for another. For instance, if you're coaching someone on your team, you might follow a pure inquiry model that presumes the individual already knows best; however, you probably would not follow that same model if you were having a difficult performance conversation.

As we've established already, it can get both confusing and time consuming when you need to pause and figure out which type of conversation you are about to have...and then ponder, compare, decide, recall, and finally select the one you might follow for that specific type of conversation. It is for this reason that the Adaptive Conversation Process is so unique and effective. Its greatest strength comes from the fact that it is "adaptable," meaning the simple step-by-step process can be used effectively, and consistently, being adapted for different types of conversations.

## HUMANS PREFER SIMPLICITY

We have heard it suggested that Leonardo da Vinci said, "simplicity is the ultimate sophistication." Business professionals and scholars alike often try to dress things up, adding fluff where it is not needed and creating frameworks that are so multifaceted it must take a huge brain and years of education to come up with such masterpieces.

The fact is that a usable process model does not need to be complicated, and sometimes too much complexity can render an idea not worth the time to figure it out. We've seen it time and time again. Simply put, humans prefer simplicity and will choose to avoid complexity whenever an alternative is present.

We have worked with many companies over the last twenty-plus years, in conventional leadership roles as well as through consulting relationships, and while approaches to business challenges differ from one company to the next, one constant seems to be the following:

**Keep it simple or people won't use it.**

Designing the simplest, effectively complete conversational progression was our goal in creating the Adaptive Conversation Process. It contains five linear steps, making it straightforward and easy to follow.

## AN OUTLINE MAKES ACTIVE LISTENING EASIER

It is important to realize that, at its core, a conversation process is committed to the idea that two-way dialogue exists for ultimate success. That's not to say a leader must engage in debate, particularly in cases where important information must be shared and/or in situations where the leader expects absolute change to result from the conversation. It does, however, infer that a conversation is not one-sided, and active listening is critical to an effective discussion.

One of the most difficult things we have heard many leaders share when confronted with the need to have a formal conversation with a team member is that sometimes, listening quality goes down the more you want to say.

Have you ever been in the middle of a conversation with someone, and suddenly caught yourself wondering what the other person just said? With the exception of day-dreaming due to a boring interaction, more times than not this is due to the fact that you are already beginning to form the basis of what you might say next, so much so that you inadvertently forget to listen to what is actually said by the other person. Leaders don't do this on purpose, but it happens all the time. Instead of constantly trying to think about what you might say next or where the conversation might need to go, the Adaptive Conversation Process provides five specific stops along the way at which you can progress through the conversation. This way, you can actively listen and engage in meaningful conversation. At any point if you start to feel a little lost along the way, you can simply look at which step in the process you are at and refocus specifically within that step, actively listening for whatever it is that step is meant to uncover, share, explore, or confirm. This grounds you to the intent of what was just said, and what you want or need to say next, along the path of an effective conversation progression.

The process is essentially your outline for the conversation, and helps you avoid drifting off or losing your place. Drift is a concept that refers to slowly getting off-track or moving from one point or stage in a conversation to another unintentionally and seemingly without control. By following a process, you know what stage in the conversation you are at, and you can intentionally move to the next step when ready instead of drifting away or just hoping you get there.

The Adaptive Conversation Process allows you to be present in the conversation, actively listen to the other person, and have an anchor to refer to by simply asking yourself, "at what step in the process is our conversation currently?"

## AN ANCHOR IN A SEA OF CHANGE

While the Adaptive Conversation Process provides a single progression for your conversations, it does not require that you forego your pre-existing philosophical frameworks, whose tenets you may have adhered to over time. For instance, if you are an executive coach certified in a particular method then you are not going to suddenly decide that the foundations you ascribe to must change dramatically - and we are not advocating for that. We too have completed formal study in multiple coaching methodologies, and we ascribe to their precepts still today. What we are saying here is that we can still be true to the tenets of those methodologies and use the Adaptive Conversation Process as a guide for conversational progression.

Some methodologies suggest a dialogue process, whereas others do not. Your comfort, style, and success as a leader are an accumulation of all you experience and learn as you grow professionally. Holistic leadership development comes from taking it all in, considering the value in many approaches, trying things on for size, putting forth the time and effort required to learn and get comfortable with something new, and deciding what works best for you. This is also what makes the Adaptive Conversation Process so useful.

Do you remember when you finished high school and people started asking what you wanted to do for your career? Maybe you went off to college and counselors asked what major you were interested in pursuing. Perhaps you went on to a post-secondary school and earned a degree in one profession only to find yourself pulled into another. There is a very good chance that over the years you have found yourself working in an industry different from the one you started in, and even in a different role than you were in five, ten, or twenty years ago.

We experience something interesting over the course of our growth as leaders. We learn, try, discuss, adjust, share, research, discover, debate, add, subtract, relearn, succeed, and fail a thousand times across our leadership journeys. The one constant is change. We have all heard that adage countless times, so it stands to reason that over the course of many years we will pick up new skills and approaches to how we converse with our team members, and we will almost certainly make changes in how we coach, and mentor, and counsel, and teach...you get the idea.

Across this long span of time in your leadership journey you will adhere to certain methodologies and almost surely you will shift to others, but along the way the Adaptive Conversation Process is your anchor in a sea of change that provides space for your methodology of choice, while serving as a simple, efficient, and effective guide for the conversation.

## A PROVEN FRAMEWORK FOR SUCCESS

The Adaptive Conversation Process is not just a theoretical model. It reflects the practical conversation techniques we have used throughout our careers as consultants, team leaders, executives, and colleagues to lead organizations, foster inclusion, and drive change. Whether overseeing billion-dollar business units, advising military leadership, or coaching emerging leaders, the principles of clarifying purpose, calling out the situation, considering possibilities, calibrating change, and committing to act have been integral in our approach to conversations and business.

From navigating complex mergers to leading global transformation initiatives, we have seen how structured conversations can unlock innovation, drive performance, and build cohesive, purpose-driven teams. The Adaptive Conversation Process can be applied to many different types of conversations, and is flexible across industries and professions, making it an essential tool for leaders who are committed to effective conversations and who aim to create lasting, positive change.

Our hope is that this process serves as a pragmatic guide, empowering you to lead with clarity, engage in meaningful dialogue, and drive measurable results - just as it has for us throughout our careers.

# 1.1

# Common Conversations

## CONVERSATIONS MAKE A DIFFERENCE

Leadership, along with the meetings and conversations we have daily, is about so much more than what we could possibly address between the covers of a single book. One thing, however, is certain - a big part of what we do as leaders is have conversations with our team members. We talk about goals and where we are going as a team. We talk about expectations and what people want for themselves and for their families. We talk about performance and how things are going along the way. We talk about learning new things and developing intentionally. We talk about our own experiences, and we share thoughts and perspectives.

There's something special about dialogue with people on our teams.

Whether we realize it in the moment or not, the conversations we have make a difference. Our teams look to us for guidance, modeling, and for direction. They may not expect all the answers, but they expect that when they talk with us, we know how to have the right conversations. It is not just about saying the right things or asking the right questions. It is, importantly, about how we engage in that dialogue with our folks because the conversations we have, and how we go about them, genuinely make a difference. How we lead a conversation can be a special thing that confirms the bond of resonance; however, if not executed properly it can confirm other feelings & assumptions held by your team member – positive or negative – about the true nature of your intent.

## WHERE YOU HAVE CONTROL

Of course, we as confident leaders don't enter a conversation expecting anything less than a great interaction. We don't wake up one morning and say, "I think

I'll really screw things up in my meetings today." By the same token, there is a saying that we have all heard before - one that a friend of ours says every other time we see him or speak on the phone about his suite of landscaping, irrigation, and pest control businesses. He says (as a rhetorical reminder), "fail to plan - plan to fail."

We have a duty to ourselves, to our team members, and to the larger organization. That duty is to be intentional and plan for how we will have meaningful conversations with our people. We call them "our people," which is an inferred sentiment that we care about them, so it stands to reason that we would not be so reckless as to assume an important conversation will just go well without effort ahead of time. As we have established, planning ahead starts with knowing what kind of conversation you are about to have, and thinking about how you will progress through that conversation.

All the methodologies in the world cannot prepare you unequivocally for how a person will react in a conversation. You can guess, and in many cases, you probably have a good idea if a conversation might go well or could go south. Your gut as a leader is certainly something to trust, but you still prepare for the unknown because you want the conversation to, at a minimum, achieve the intended outcome. This is where the Adaptive Conversation Process becomes your trusted guide and comes in extremely handy. The bits and pieces of dialogue may change and swerve into unexpected corners, and you will not always have control over where the other person goes; however, if your conversational progression is established in advance, you have more control over where you take the discussion regardless of anything else.

Before we dive into the specific steps of the Adaptive Conversation Process, let us first explore a few of the most common types of conversations leaders are faced with regularly. These are not the only types of conversations this process model can be used to guide you through; however, they seem to come up very often, so it helps to use them as examples in understanding how the Adaptive Conversation Process works.

## COACHING AND MENTORING

Coaching and mentoring are often used broadly to refer to intentionally helping another toward development.

First, there is coaching and mentoring that is driven largely by the leader, which is usually borne of the need to help an employee get better at something identified by the leader or company as important for job or task success. This reference is more closely related to "teaching" or "training." We hear all the time about how leaders must set aside time to coach their team members, and often we find that it is around skills or competencies identified by the leader as developmental needs to achieve something or to elevate results. This is not entirely what true coaching is all about. While not conventionally the most exact definition (especially if you ask a devout leadership coach), it is still widely used to describe these types of conversations. If defined in this way - even in part - by enough leaders, then it is happening, and we think it is appropriate to acknowledge it as a kind of coaching conversation that does take place. This is why having a structured process for the conversation becomes even more important.

The second way to look at coaching and mentoring is that which is driven by the employee – not the leader. It is still borne of the need for development, though it places the employee in the driver's seat and engages the leader in a position to guide an open and probing conversation.

In this way, we would more acutely define coaching as a leader partnering in a conversational process to inspire growth in another through inquiry and open thought processes along a path of self-discovery to achieve intentional change/goals. It is less about teaching how to do something different or better (as important as the skill or competency may be to job success), and more about helping the employee explore something, however overtly or subconsciously known, which is important to the individual's own goals for development. If you are a certified coach, or even if you are seasoned enough to have followed any number of coaching models, you have likely engaged in coaching conversations and have become adept at asking open-ended, probing questions that help that other person to explore his or her feelings and ideas, opening perspectives and possibilities that could lead to intended development and growth.

Mentoring, although like coaching, is different in that its intent is for someone with seasoned experience to share it with another, in a formal and intentional manner over time through meaningful ongoing dialogue, which helps the other person on his or her path for change and growth. While coaching helps someone explore their own feelings and ideas on the road to development, mentoring intentionally taps into the feelings and experiences of the mentor as a vehicle for sharing on the road to development. If you have ever truly mentored someone, you have probably been asked to share your background and tell stories of how you approached or accomplished something to achieve success. The person you are mentoring is interested in learning from your experiences, and eager to get a flavor for what you have been exposed to. Through this type of conversation, direct learning and new perspectives that come from those shared experiences can lead to development and often deep professional relationships.

## PERFORMANCE-RELATED

If coaching and mentoring refer largely to conversations around new perspectives for changing and developing something that has yet to be achieved, then performance-related conversations – in some circumstances even referred to as performance counseling - can be characterized as the opposite.

When an employee has shown competence or success and achievement in an area, and then backslides in performance or fails to achieve expectations, a performance-related conversation may be necessary. Leaders often characterize these as "performance discussions" or "difficult employee conversations." However they are positioned, they intend to acknowledge something that is not currently as it needs to be and then come up with a direction for the underperforming individual to achieve expectations or get back to the success once demonstrated.

Performance appraisals and regularly scheduled reviews are only part of what these types of conversations represent. If you have been a people-leader for more than a minute, then you have likely already learned that your team members should never be surprised when you have a performance-related conversation. This is why many organizations have implemented regularly scheduled performance check-ins, and some have even moved away from annual appraisals altogether replacing them with ongoing performance discussions and milestones. If you ensure people know what is expected of them, and you communicate often so they know where they stand in relation to that expectation, then the conversation you might need to have should be easier and almost expected.

Additionally, performance-related conversations do not only mean telling someone they are falling short. If performance can be subpar, then it can also be exceeding. These types of conversations also occur on a healthy team, and seasoned leaders know to make enough positive deposits in acknowledging this if they are to succeed when the more difficult conversations must take place. A pat on the back does not equally offset a formal conversation around performance shortfalls, and since all leaders forget sometimes how important it is to formally recognize and discuss achievements regularly, it is the difficult performance conversation that makes most leaders squint their eyes and sometimes even wait too long to have it.

Of course, these types of conversations may be progressive in what they include, as repeated conversations may advance to include things like promotions on the positive side, or performance improvement plans on the other; however, from a process perspective the conversational progression and overall intent remains consistent.

## CONSULTING AND ADVISING

According to Peter Block, whenever you offer advice to someone faced with a choice, you are consulting. Whether doing so with the intent to influence another, or in response to a request for advice or best practice, leaders consult (advise) their team members as well as countless others across the organization.

For conversations with team members, the leader is often faced with an expectation of some freedom of choice on how to get a job done, yet often still provide some guidance and/or rails within which to operate and achieve expectations. Leaders are constantly asked by team members for advice. "How would you approach this? How have we done it in the past? What's the best way, or what might work here?" These are some of the questions our people ask us all the time. Most leaders have regular one-on-one meetings with their team members, and often this is when questions such as these come up. A team member is having a difficult time figuring out how to move a project forward or how to get something done, so he or she asks the leader for advice, and depending on the full context of the issue and relationship, a consultative approach may certainly be the appropriate conversation.

For conversations with clients (whether internal or external customers) the same holds true, with the added expectation that the leader may bring an elevated level of expertise that can be considered in solving a problem or crafting a solution for something specific for which they are engaging together. For instance, a client may be experiencing a challenge and simply need to talk through finding an answer. Likewise, a coworker might simply want to have a conversation around ideas to improve or deliver something in a different way for which you bring specific expertise. As for your team members, they too may want to engage you in conversation to brainstorm based on what you know that they do not. Others we work with and serve rely on us to be the ones who know certain things, and the conversations they expect may be around options and alternatives, with guidance to achieve their ends.

Regardless of the situation or audience, at a high level the conversation is largely the same. It is a relationship hinged on the expectation of expertise or capability, and it is deliberately collaborative.

## CHANGE

There is an abundance of literature and research that has been done around change - both leading it and managing it. Leaders have the distinct challenge of sitting in a position to lead change, while they too are expected to go through it just like anyone else, and they are expected to manage it both in process and from a human-side perspective.

Change conversations tend to fall into more than one bucket, so we'll focus on two types: (1) those relating to communicating the change itself, and (2) those surrounding the effect change has on people.

In our experience, leaders find it much easier to have conversations around the former than the latter. If something is changing, the leader can play a critical role in communicating details to his or her team. When will the change take place? How will it be rolled out? What will we do differently? What will the new process be? How do we do it? You get the idea. In the end, people need to know things so communication around the change itself usually comes across as informative and necessary.

Conversations around the human side of change and the effect it has on people can be much more difficult, though they are just as important if not more so. Why are we changing? Why now? How will this truly impact my work? What is really in it for me? Can I learn the new way? How will I learn it? Can I do it as well as I did before? Can I be successful in the new way? How will it feel? Can I keep it up? There are many models for addressing the human side of change, and we are not going to address them in this book; rather, it is important to recognize that these are conversations we must have with people as their leader, and a structured conversation process can be extremely helpful.

## TEACHING AND TRAINING

As a leader, you probably do a fair amount of teaching or training for your team members. From the time new employees join your team, they look to you for the information and abilities they need to do the job as you expect it to be done. They look to you for answers they do not yet know. They turn to you when they do something wrong, or at least not as well as could have been done, and they expect you will be able to show them a better way. In a nutshell, they look to you to enable their success.

It is very common for leaders to refer to teaching and training as coaching; however, as we have established, there is a difference. When coaching, you are "passively teaching" by helping guide another person on a path to self-discovery. When teaching or training, you have the answers and are sharing them with that other person. There may be elements of coaching, mentoring, or advising along the way, but a conversation meant to teach something is unique in and of itself.

One critical thing to remember when having such a conversation is that you are working with adults; therefore, it is different than when you learned something in school. When you were in high school or college, teachers had the information, and you took what they said as "truth" because you had nothing else to go on. It was all new and no real context existed. Conversely, as an adult you have a wealth of experience to draw from and bump new learning up against. This is a critical difference (from an academic perspective, it is the primary difference between pedagogy and andragogy).

Successful teaching and training conversations must consider the entirety of a person's background and allow for a comparison of what is being taught to what has already been experienced in the past. This is why following the Adaptive Conversation Process as an intentional conversation progression is often much easier with adults. They have something real and meaningful to pull from when they are asked questions and guided down the path of active learning. Things usually make more sense when a contextual picture can be painted.

One more important thing to note about teaching and training conversations is that adults tend to drive their learning, so the conversation itself, if moving in a reasonable direction, will be sufficient to engage the person. A prevailing theory in adult education, established by Malcolm Knowles, is a fundamental truth that adults self-direct their learning; therefore, teaching or training conversations need only progress in a meaningful and understandable way to expect engagement and success.

# 1.2

# Overview: The Adaptive Conversation Process

## KEEP IT SIMPLE

While every leader, and organization for that matter, is different there is a common theme that emerges consistently when trying a new approach or implementing a new process: keep it simple. Complexity can be the biggest obstacle to success. The Adaptive Conversation Process is intentionally simple, making its use in the real world understandable, readily accessible for every leader faced with an impending conversation, and applicable in many situations, particularly for the most common types of conversations.

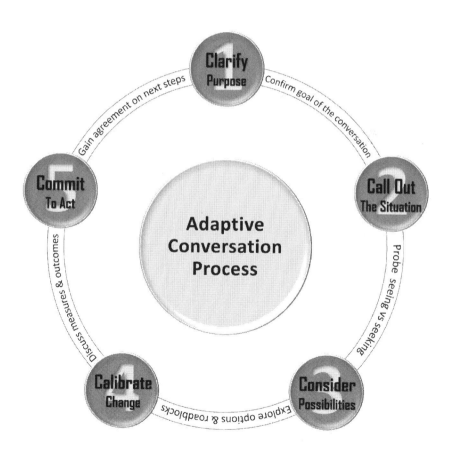

## CLARIFY PURPOSE

How often have you sat down for a conversation with an employee, only to find that five minutes into the talk the two of you are not on the same page?

All too often, leaders get so preoccupied with what their general intent for the conversation is, that they go too fast and skip right past making sure the purpose of the conversation is clear to the other person. As the leader, you already know what you want to ask or say. You already know what you believe to be true about the conversation. You already have an idea about what the other person might say or might want to talk about. You may have already deconstructed whatever it is that you heard or observed and made sense of it based on your understanding and past experiences.

Then the biggest mistake happens...and you move forward in the conversation before making sure you and the other person are on the same page.

After several minutes, typically in mid-sentence, you realize this has occurred because you see a somewhat blank stare on the face of your team member. It is the strained and confused look that says, "Wait...what are we talking about and why?" You pause to check, maybe even probing for understanding, and sure enough your team member is struggling to figure out exactly what you are asking, why you are going down a certain path, what kind of conversation is happening, and even more importantly where it is going.

You quickly reverse direction and go backwards so you might both get on the same page, and then when you feel you are on track you try and remember where you were going in the first place. You get that, "let's start over" feeling and some of the conversation's luster has surely worn off before you could even get it going.

Wouldn't things be simpler if you just focused on ensuring that your purpose for the conversation was clarified right from the start? Would it help to have one objective up front: Validate the purpose of the conversation? That's it, first.

Rather than thinking about every bit of the conversation, just focus up front on step one in the Adaptive Conversation Process, which is Clarify Purpose.

If you let yourself be concerned about how the rest of the conversation will go, then you risk getting it started in the wrong direction right from the beginning.

Have you ever backed your car out of the driveway only to realize that you pointed yourself in the wrong direction? You probably paused for a moment, squeezed your eyes shut realizing the mistake you made, and then decided what to do next. Did you pull back in the driveway and back out again pointing the other way, or did you just go with it and turn yourself around on another street. Both options work, but either way you started out wrong and either impacted your mental readiness or took a longer route.

The most important thing at first is not to worry about what your team member might say. Can you control what someone else says, or thinks, or needs? Can you decide for another person what they will decide to say when you ask, "what would you like to talk about today," or "Do you know why we needed a few minutes together," or "How can I make this better or more understandable for you?" You cannot effectively move forward unless you first confirm the purpose of the conversation. At the onset of a conversation, the only thing that matters is starting out well...not the rest of the dialogue...so be specific and clear up front and you will set a path for a successful conversation.

## CALL OUT THE SITUATION

If you are having a conversation with one of your team members, then it is probably for good reasons and something that matters to you both. The conversation is relevant, so it stands to reason that your first point of order in the conversational progression after ensuring clarity is to call out the situation. Now, when we say "call out" we do not mean to question validity; rather, we are talking about acknowledging the situation as it stands today and laying it transparently on the table. If it is a coaching conversation, then you might want to paint a picture of how things are going now compared to how your team members might like to see them change. If it is a performance conversation, perhaps it is important to make clear what behavior is occurring presently compared to what the preferred behavior should be. These examples help illustrate how calling out the situation is helpful.

When laying out facts at two ends of a continuum – with "what you are seeing" in the current state at one end, and "what you are seeking" in an expected state at the other end, placement on that continuum becomes clearer, gaps begin to rise to the surface, and outcome differentials can be explored for potential impacts. Differential impact provides further clarity and becomes validated justification for the conversation itself.

Have you ever sat down for a conversation with your leader, been very clear on the specific purpose of the conversation, yet you felt a little fuzzy about the value of the conversation anyway? Or maybe the value of the conversation was clear at first but after a few minutes you start to get the idea that it is about to go down a different path? You probably got those feelings because your leader failed to call out the situation in a transparent way that made the conversation's path forward clear. Conversely, if your leader did a good job with this, then you probably found yourself sharing easily, nodding your head in agreement, and ready for the next question or statement in the dialogue.

When you have a conversation with team members, look into their eyes. If you see them glazing over a little, with their head at a slight tilt, you may still have work to do in this step. Likewise, if your team members are still talking a lot, it probably means there is more to call out so do not rush through this step. If you see a mutual understanding forming behind their eyes as their head begins to nod and the dialogue seems to slow down, you are probably ready to move forward in the conversation.

## CONSIDER POSSIBILITIES

We know that types of conversations differ. Coaching is highly inquiry-based, where the leader asks probing questions. Performance dialogue is more directional and carries specific, important, time-bound intent. Mentoring is a form of shared storytelling, with questions helping lead down the right path. Teaching & training is about imparting information and engaging in dialogue for understanding and ability or competence development. Consulting is influential in response to a need for advice or best practice. While conversations vary, and sometimes technical or procedural requirements demand that there be one way to do something, in most cases one size fits all is an exception, not the norm.

In this third step, exploring possibilities is the name of the game. It is an opportunity to step back for a moment and talk out loud about what might be done to close the gap identified along the "seeing vs seeking" continuum confirmed in the prior step. It is not yet time to commit to action, but it is time to "think about possible actions." At this stage in the conversational progression, the dialogue is about a combination of discussing past behaviors and how future alternatives might be explored. If you think it sounds a lot like brainstorming hypothetically, and discussing conceptual and realistic options, then you are right on the money.

If it is an advisory type of conversation, you might ask what the current approach has yielded and offer what an alternative might produce. If it is a mentoring conversation, you may share the thought process you had in a prior experience, the options you went through, and how those might be applied in the current conversation. These examples help show the power of the mind and how speaking ideas out loud can create space for innovation and success.

Taking time to explore roadblocks adds another value-add in the conversation. What might be getting in the way of expected performance? How might a person be self-limiting based on assumptions of what is missing rather than what exists? What resources are required if the options explored are to be truly put in motion? How specifically can you as a leader support your team member's success as intended in the conversation? Roadblocks can be a barrier or a gatekeeper. They can either be the things that prevent someone from making mental possibilities a reality, or they can be acknowledged and discussed as ways to empower your people and enable progress and success.

We don't always think before we act, but usually when we do, we can expect greater results. This step gives you and your team members the time and space to create meaningful dialogue around what may (or may not) be something to do next. Ensuring ample conversational effort in this step is like creating a sort of mini-think tank. Whether the conversation indicates you should be asking more questions, giving clearer directions, or mutually exploring potential impacts, you will likely spend a good amount of time in this step.

# CALIBRATE CHANGE

Once possibilities and roadblocks in the conversation have been explored, a true bearing for action will be clear. Even after spending significant time and effort to this point, this is where many leaders find themselves unknowingly rushing to wrap things up too quickly. The problem with that is by rushing to close, just as you might expect in project management or organizational effectiveness, neglecting to fully discuss measures can derail the output expected from the conversation.

Have you ever had a conversation with one of your team members, where you felt like the stars and moon aligned while you were together, and you wrapped things up in a way that felt good to you both, only to find later that what you both expected would result just did not come to fruition? The options from the conversation simply, for one reason or another, did not work? You may have both been on the same page, pointed in the expected direction, and ready to reach whatever it was you set out to achieve in the conversation, but when you connected again you found that no meaningful progress to the goal had been made. Perhaps even steps were taken, and possibilities were acted on, yet the goal still seemed just as far away as the day you initially spoke. This may have been due to skipping over (or not spending enough intentional time) calibrating change.

Leaders, as we are all human, can fall into the trap of making assumptions. When the conversation feels good, it is even easier to fall into this trap and rush past the calibrating change step. It is too important to miss.

Let's first dig into what calibration really is. It is easy to mistake this step for only identifying strict metrics or firm outcomes. You are having a conversation about something, which may or may not be a singular determinant in an outcome. That is why the very first step in the Adaptive Conversation Process is clarifying purpose. Calibration in this case is meant to gauge to what degree options and possibilities are working. These are leading indicators that help predict achievement of the conversation's stated goals and may or may not equate to wholly established outputs. It is about taking time to discuss measures and outcomes in terms of what they mean against the specific goal of the conversation itself.

Another important element of calibration is that it does not require end-measure equality. Every option attempted, roadblock removed, possibility realized, or resource obtained may not equally impact goal achievement. Calibrating change is about exploring gradations of measuring possibilities and considering what that might mean in the achievement of the goal. Some things make a bigger difference than others, and everything is in some way interconnected. If possibilities considered in the prior step of the Adaptive Conversation Process are about exploring potential perspectives and options, then calibrating change is about predicting and establishing what the measures of those perspectives and options should look like, or yield, once applied. Consider it conversation of an incremental rubric toward the goal.

## COMMIT TO ACT

The final step in the Adaptive Conversation Process is committing to act on the options established. The gravity of this commitment, and to what degree it is driven by the leader or team member, depends on the type of conversation. Nonetheless, gaining agreement on next steps is like a conversational handshake that closes the interaction.

How did we begin the conversation? We started with clarity (of the conversation's purpose), so it is just as important to end the conversation with clarity (of what happens next and by whom). Lack of clarity around commitment can breed ambiguity and uncertainty. When leadership conversations are closed with ambiguity on what may happen next, everything up to that point in the conversation may be jeopardized, and expectations ahead can fall prey to multiple interpretations. There can be no lack of certainty about what comes next. Whether a coachee is stating what will be done first, or a leader is directing what must happen next, or a client is confirming when something specific will happen, the one constant is that commitment is verbalized, clear, and owned.

You've probably heard the clichés, "talk is cheap" and "actions speak louder than words." That is the crux of what we are aiming to address by ensuring the final step in the Adaptive Conversation Process is a commitment to act. It allows for closure in the conversation, firm ownership of what is to come, and a point of reflection against actions, measures, observations, and desires that all lead back to a stated goal.

## ADAPTABLE CONVERSATIONS AT THE HEART OF PROGRESS

Some conversations are meaty, full of substance with lots to talk about. Others are light and cover topics at a more surface level. Certain conversations carry critical personal or professional importance with impactful dialogue that can move mountains. Still others are less consequential and dance along the line of preference or perspective.

When leaders talk with direct reports, team members, peers, bosses, and even among themselves, purpose, intent, and expectations run the gamut. Progression and an end for every beginning are consistently present in every effective conversation.

As executives with decades of experience in leadership roles spanning corporate, non-profit, and entrepreneurial sectors, we have consistently relied on adaptive, structured communication to navigate complex environments. Whether leading Fortune 50 companies, advising military organizations, or growing start-ups, one constant remains: effectively adaptable conversations are at the heart of progress.

The Adaptive Conversation Process mirrors the key principles we have employed throughout our careers, helping to build high-performing teams, align organizational objectives, and achieve impactful outcomes.

# SECTION TWO:

## THE ADAPTIVE CONVERSATION PROCESS:

### *FOUR PERSONAS*

# 2.0

# The Persona Approach

# REPRESENTATIVE CHARACTERS AS EXAMPLES IN ACTION

In this book, we strive to make it easy for you to see the benefits of the Adaptive Conversation Process, a single process model that adapts to many different types of conversations.

We also want to make it easy to understand pragmatically, express how it allows room for adherence to tenets from complementary models, and show clearly what it looks like in use.

Improving your conversations does not have to be confusing or daunting; rather, it can be easy to approach and develop.

There will certainly be times when you want to step out of the box, which is understandable and ok. Learning to follow a new process of any kind takes time and practice. A long time ago, we were working with an organization on a new approach to customer service. Someone told us that it is much better to tell someone, "It is my pleasure" than to say, "No problem," a common response. That person explained that the latter response is negative and could ignore the fact that perhaps there was indeed a "problem;" therefore inadvertently discounting the gesture itself, whereas the former response is positive and can only make someone feel good. We started using this more positive response for everything from delivery on service, to opening the door when clients came to the office. For a while, it felt uncomfortable and clunky. As time went on, it started to feel normal. Today, it has become second nature. The same goes for using the Adaptive Conversation Process. It may feel uncomfortable at first as you look down at your notes and refrain from bouncing around in different parts of the conversation. In time and with personal and professional commitment to it, however, you will find that it feels normal, and eventually it will become second nature, improving your conversations and their outcomes.

To help ground the Adaptive Conversation Process, making it a bit easier to understand, we will introduce you to four characters – personas – to join us on this learning journey. Personas serve as characters, grounded as real-life people who are realistic and representative of people we engage with. They can help us become more aware of ourselves and others we engage with as we discuss the Adaptive Conversation Process. They help us see the benefit and impact of this process model in action, through distinct illustration. They help us to connect to the need for the Adaptive Conversation Process, as well as how and when it can be helpful in real-life interactions. They also assist in recognizing what it really looks like for people just like us.

We hope that these unique and diverse personas will serve as helpful guides on your learning journey. We will introduce you to them now, and they will pop back up throughout the book as we move through the five stages of the Adaptive Conversation Process. While they all hold unique roles, at different levels and in various industries, they have one thing in common. They all experienced different types of conversations, which were made better by following the Adaptive Conversation Process. As you get to know them, you will likely see elements of yourself or someone you know. Take time to connect with our characters – these personas – and as you practice using the Adaptive Conversation Process, recall how it helped them along the way as it may very well help you from reading their stories.

Please allow us to introduce you to Molly, Carter, Ezra, and Olivia.

# 2.1
# Persona #1
# Molly, VP of Lending

## MOLLY, VICE PRESIDENT OF LENDING

Ice cold sweet tea, the birthplace of Dr. Martin Luther King Jr., rush-hour traffic you do not want to be caught in, seventy-one streets with "Peachtree" in their name and most sarcastically referred to as "Hotlanta," the bustling greater Atlanta, Georgia metropolitan area is where Molly has always called home.

Born and raised just 30 miles outside the city center, in the northeastern suburb of Snellville, Molly grew up smack dab in the heart of middle-class America. Her father was a mid-level manager in the advertising industry, working sixty-plus hours a week to provide semi-comfortable living for the family, while her mother stayed home raising her along with three siblings. Sure, dad was the bread winner, and the family was rarely in need of food, clothing, or the necessities in life, but Molly knew who provided the "extras." You see, mom was always doing some sort of business from the house. Whether selling kitchen wares, making holiday decorations for neighbors and friends, or coordinating some sort of community event, she seemed to have her hands in two or three things at once so she could sock-away fifty bucks here and a hundred dollars there for weekend getaways in the nearby Smoky Mountains or downtown for the night at a restaurant that showed up as $$$ instead of $. More than anything, she really taught Molly about work that matters and how to value money.

In high school, Molly always did well - not amazing, but well. She studied hard when she needed to and was a people-person through and through, although she also did her share of partying. Her friends always laughed and said she must take after her daddy because she was the treasurer and events coordinator of the school's spirit club, and she was always on the homecoming and prom dance committees in charge of ticket sales and budgeting. Between dad being a businessman and mom being a home-based entrepreneur, people just figured Molly would end up at some big firm in downtown Atlanta. After high school she took a gap-year and spent a lot of time doing community service. Eventually those high school expectations moved her to enroll in college, where she graduated in four and a half years with a degree in Economics...and that is when the world of assumption was introduced to the world of reality.

Two weeks after graduation, Molly got that job everyone said she would get, working at a startup wealth-management agency downtown, engaged in the business-side of individual investments. It was fun at first, but that new job allure wore off quickly amid 60-hour work weeks, many in the car going from house-to-house meetings with individuals and families. One year later, the startup could not stay afloat and shut down, leaving Molly back on the job market. Not quite sure of her next move, she reached out to her alma mater and signed up for career coaching assistance provided through the university's Alumni Career Services office. A bright, in-state collegiate graduate, she found another job very quickly, this time at a local investment firm with a long history in business, serving as a Corporate Investment Processor. Having found new employment, she ended her career coaching with the university, assuming it had become unnecessary, even though sessions never really got much further than talking about her current graduate and employment experience. This new job was different in that she had a cubicle and sometimes found herself visiting clients in high-rise buildings in the heart of Atlanta. Like the first job, it was fun at first, but the pace was faster than she could have imagined. Molly was smart, but as she acclimated to this new role, she floundered a bit, finding herself having difficult performance conversations from time to time with her boss, and learning that she had more development to do than she even thought. She had her ups and downs with the company, and when a year flew by like a day, she found herself once again on the outside looking in when her department downsized her right out of a job.

Molly felt a flurry of emotions - sadness, disappointment, confusion, anger, shame, and more. She was too embarrassed to reach back out to her former career coach at the university, and she had not held a job long enough to feel comfortable reaching back to a former boss for guidance. Luckily for Molly, mom's side-hustles were still booming, and she connected with a family friend who owned a real estate firm just outside the city in Marietta. He had just lost his Investments Specialist. Without a second thought, she found herself in her third job in three years, going in with optimism and fingers crossed.

Fast forward three more years, and life was good – not great, but good. Molly was skilled at her job and always met or exceeded expectations in her performance reviews, but something was missing. On the anniversary of her third year with the firm, and after working in the investments arena for five or six years by now, Molly came to a difficult decision – she simply did not love what she was doing, spending more time with numbers than people, and she wanted a change. She confided in her boss, sharing her true feelings while being careful not to imply that she was ready to quit. Molly was fortunate, as her boss knew the value of coaching and immediately asked her if she was interested in having regular conversations that might help sort out these feelings and the next steps. She started having formally scheduled talks with her boss once every two weeks, and within six months she put in her notice and left for a new job at a community bank within bike riding distance from her apartment.

Starting as a branch teller, Molly learned the ropes from the ground up, and absolutely loved engaging with people from the community, some of whom she knew from the volunteering work she continued to do on weekends. She advanced to a role in Account Services, then to Loan Clerk and Universal Representative. When the community bank was acquired by a larger regional bank, one of her volunteer friends told her about an opening for a Loan Processor on her team at the credit union she worked at, so Molly applied and was hired on the spot. By now, she knew the value of connecting with someone for the purpose of learning, growing and engaging in coaching conversations. At first her boss served in this capacity for her but as she rose up in the ranks, she formed a solid relationship with a director who had also started at the credit union as a teller. Fifteen years later, now married with two children of her own, Molly – economics major turned credit union industry leader – is the Vice President of Lending for that very same credit union.

The credit union has always placed a premium on learning and development, so over the years Molly learned a lot as a leader. She learned about building resonant relationships with her team members and with others across the organization. She learned about the hallmarks of good leadership, how leading people differs from managing them, and the importance of organizational savvy. She developed competencies related to emotional intelligence and fine-tuned a variety of skills in a blended manner though everything from coursework to intentional experiences and more. One thing, however, that always seemed most complex was the art and science of having effective conversations with her team members. Molly put in the effort to learn about several models, frameworks, and approaches to being successful in leading different types of discussions, but since every person and situation is different, she often struggled with knowing which model to use...for which type of conversation...and hoped the dialogue did not shift unexpectedly midstream. She struggled and often would leave a conversation wondering if she was clear enough, or asked the right questions, or set expectations. All those years of experience and development helped, but there was still something about conversations that made them difficult from one situation to the next. Then, she learned about the Adaptive Conversation Process, and everything changed for the better.

In the chapters that follow, we'll explore some of Molly's experiences. We will see the impact using the Adaptive Conversation Process had, not only on how she grew as a leader but also how she learned to shift from one conversation type to another using this single conversation process.

# 2.2
# Persona #2
# Carter, Nursing Director
# (USAF Retired)

## Carter, Nursing Director (USAF Retired)

Grandpa Charlie gave commands in a six-month campaign, leading naval air forces from a carrier in the Pacific Theater during the Battle of Guadalcanal, in the pursuit of controlling the Solomon Islands. Uncle Stewart fought along the 38th parallel in the Korean War, and dad flew a C-47 Gooney Bird back and forth between Thailand and Vietnam for eighteen months from 1967-1969. With a sister serving as a medic on two tours in the middle east, and a cousin serving in the Marines leading an amphibious infantry unit, Carter started on his military path early in life. As a child, he used to set up toy army men in the flower beds in his Suburban, Ohio backyard and spent hours pretending to be a medic saving little green plastic lives. For a while in middle school, he thought he might want to be a veterinarian, but that was short-lived as most adults in his family had served in the military and he already knew what he wanted to be when he grew up. He even knew the title he aspired to: Chief Master Sergeant, leading a team of Aerospace Medical Service Specialists. Sure enough, Carter graduated from high school with honors and, after four years of AFROTC at the university, he joined the United States Air Force and continued his medical training.

Carter was a people-person through and through. In college, he joined a fraternity. It was not something he planned or even knew much about before freshman year, but when his dorm room neighbor invited him to a party at the fraternity house one night, he made fast friends. The next morning four guys showed up at his dorm and handed him a formal invitation to "rush" and get to know the members. He enjoyed his time at college, his studies, fraternity life, and his ROTC coursework and leadership laboratories. Carter always looked up to one of his older fraternity brothers who seemed wise beyond his years, often repeating quotes he shared with Carter like, "Cast your bread upon the waters, for you will find it after many days," or "The wind does not wait for the tree to bend." Sometimes when Carter was having a rough week, he would sit down with his buddy for a bit of advice, and it would usually help a great deal.

Being part of ROTC was important in Carter's development as a growing young man and as a future leader. Learning Labs gave him opportunities to solve problems, take initiative, and lead others – not from a place of power alone but from a place of empathy and authentic communication. The Major in charge of the program took an interest in him. They would often see each other around campus and would always end up walking together for a while. Carter did not realize it at the time, but those walks were so much more than the passing of time or simply getting from point A to point B. They were mini-mentoring sessions, as the Major himself graduated from the university's ROTC program many years back, and he had a gift for sharing his experiences in ways that made sense to young men and women. Carter flew through his first two years in the program, excelled in completing field training at Lackland Air Force Base in San Antonio, Texas and signed his final USAF paperwork when he graduated college, moving onto the next phase of his career with excitement and passion.

The United States military is well known for developing great leaders, and this was certainly true for Carter. It was in the U.S. Air Force where he would continue the study and practice of medicine, get married, have two children, and surpass his childhood goal of Chief Master Sergeant (since he was a commissioned officer). After twenty years he retired from military service practicing medicine with the rank of Lieutenant Colonel and moved into his second career – as the Nursing Director for a small hospital in the Midwest.

One of the most interesting parts of being in a hospital for Carter was the pace of work. There were certainly times when the nature of medical service necessitated speed and even a bit of controlled chaos, but by and large things were often slower than he was used to in the military. He mostly attributed that to the smaller size of the hospital he chose, but nonetheless things often moved at a quiet to moderate clip – and this was exactly the right pace to find ample opportunity for meaningful conversations with his teams. Carter loved teaching, but most people knew about his military past and enjoyed hearing how his experiences led him to achieve much of what they themselves were looking for. It seemed that every month he had someone asking if he would be their mentor. Whether it was improving communication skills, building relationships, or navigating a sea of career choices folks at the hospital rarely asked him, "what would you do;" instead, they would say, "Tell me about your experience with that." Carter did not mind one bit.

Leadership is a tricky thing for many, but for Carter it was ingrained in him from a very early age, and he knew that shared experiences were one of the many important ways he could add value for others - in their work and in their lives. He has outlasted several travelling nurses at the hospital, not to mention countless transporters and other techs coming straight out of school who eventually left for larger medical facilities around the country. For Carter, he is still right where he wants to be – leading a team of nurses who make a difference in people's lives every day. He meets them "where they are" in their development and engages with them in ways that matter. A few times he has been asked to make a shift from his role as Nursing Director and to become Chief of Staff to the CEO, and each time he respectfully declines the opportunity maintaining his "current tour" of making a difference in the growth of the nurses on his team.

Many folks have asked Carter why retirement (from the military) for him meant going to work, and why he chose the role he did at a small hospital when a retired Lieutenant Colonel could easily vie for the role of Chief Nursing Officer at any big metropolitan hospital. He would always respond in the same way: "Cast your bread upon the waters, for you will find it after many days." Carter has learned so much over the years – from his time in the fraternity, to his walks with the Major, to his career in the Air Force. He cast his bread a long time ago, and if there were crumbs to be found he wanted to pass along some of what he had learned to others finding their way in the medical field.

As we make our way through this book, we will visit again with Carter and see how application of the Adaptive Conversation Process helped him as a leader, and as a guide for so many.

# 2.3
# Persona #3
# Ezra, Director of Sales

# EZRA, DIRECTOR OF SALES

An entrepreneurial spirit, an out-of-the-box thinker, a true salesman, and a people-person. These are all ways Ezra has been described by anyone who got to know him for more than a few days. His personality for talking with people and making things happen started at a young age.

Growing up in a working-class family in an eastern suburb of Cleveland, Ohio, Ezra yearned for more in life and knew one day he would make money, earn success, and change lives. He dreamt big. One Friday evening while eating dinner with his parents and two sisters, Ezra asked for $10 to go with his friends to the local community days festival that kicked off that weekend. Tired from a long day at work as a maintenance electrician, his father looked at him and said, "son if you want to be rich, go sell something." Little did his dad know how impactful that statement would be for Ezra, right then and later in life.

A couple weeks later Ezra went to the local bulk foods store with his mother. Walking through the aisles and tasting free samples was always fun, but on that day, Ezra was up to something. He made his way over to an aisle filled with snack bars and candies, and an idea took shape. Ezra was only in seventh grade at this time, but his innate gift as an entrepreneur and salesman were about to be on full display. The following weekend, with his mother's help, he purchased one box of gum-filled lollipops that came in a variety of flavors (sour apple was his favorite). When he went home, he sat down and figured out very quickly that to make a good profit he would need to sell each lollipop for 25 cents. One box had 100 lollipops in it, and the whole box only cost $6 to buy, giving him a profit of $19 per box. His plan was set, and he was ready to see everyone at school that coming week.

Once word got out that Ezra was selling lollipops from his locker, he sold out in the first fifteen minutes of lunch period.

The next week he brought in two boxes and sold them out within days. Things carried on like this for months until the administration of the school noticed every other kid walking around with a lollipop in their mouth and getting to classes late while stopping off at Ezra's locker first. Now, no one ever told him directly but when the announcement was broadcast over the loudspeaker that students were not allowed to sell unauthorized items during school hours, he knew his dream of being a candy baron was over, for the moment.

The following year, the school's athletic booster club was doing an official fundraiser selling candy bars for the season, and on the back of each wrapper was a coupon for a free candy bar. The candy business was back on! Throughout the day as kids ate their fundraiser bars, Ezra would grab their wrappers before they could toss them in the trash. He even spoke with the custodians after school and picked up wrappers swept up in the halls. Each week he collected about 100 wrappers that had been tossed away, which meant he was entitled to a hundred free candy bars, every week. Ezra leaned on his communication and relationship-building skills and got to know the owner of the local convenience store who let him select a variety of candy bars with those coupons. This time, he didn't sneak around selling in the school. Instead, he went door to door, selling his candy as a "fund-raiser" and not a fundraiser. He never lied as he made his way around the neighborhood. He always told the truth and explained that a kid his age needed to find ways to make money, and all he was doing was putting in the work to collect coupons while pounding the pavement to sell his product – and people ate that up (literally and figuratively).

His entrepreneurial spirit and interpersonal savvy helped him through college and then onto his first job for a large cruise line. Every day in the back of his mind he could hear his dad saying, "If you want to make money, go sell something" and that's exactly what he did. It was no surprise to anyone when he was presented with the Five-Diamond Award, which recognized the top salesperson in the entire company. After accepting for the third year in a row, while at an annual travel sales conference in Las Vegas, he ran into the SVP of Operations for a big Hotel and Casino. They met a year prior, and she always marveled at how easily Ezra navigated a room, seeming to make everyone feel like his best friend instantly and like they were the most important person in the world at that moment. Her sales manager was leaving for a new job, and she was given carte blanche on finding a replacement. She wasted no time and asked if Ezra was interested in the position. More money, a company vehicle, and all the expenses one would expect with a cross-country move would be taken care of. Ezra smiled from ear to ear, thought again about his dad, and accepted the job.

As Ezra's tenure grew at the Hotel and Casino, so did his position as he found himself accepting the role of Director of Sales. From his working-class family beginnings, he had certainly grown and accomplished everything he hoped for. Things were easy...until he had to truly manage the performance of all those salespeople that he used to work alongside. That took another set of skills, and required very different kinds of conversations from the ones he was used to having with the team when his most challenging work was showing new hires how it was done. For the first time in his career everything was not as easy as it once was.

As you progress through this book, you will join Ezra on his growth in leadership and hear about how he used the Adaptive Conversation Process to navigate conversations.

# 2.4

# Persona #4

# Olivia, Director of IT (CISSP, PMP)

## OLIVIA, DIRECTOR OF INFORMATION TECHNOLOGY (CISSP, PMP)

It was 7:05am when the bell rang, which made Ms. Olivia jump and nearly spill her fresh cup of coffee on her lap. Still trying to get songs from her iTunes account over to her new laptop did not seem to be as easy as her students explained, but it was time for class. She stood up and called Sophia, one of her students, to come to help quickly. Instead of doing it for her, Sophia gave her three concise instructions – to which the steps led to success. Easy-peasy. Ms. Olivia joked, "Thanks Professor," and Sophia took her seat with a smile. That was the first thing Olivia reflected on after leaving her job as a high school teacher and starting her very first "real IT job" as a Helpdesk Coordinator in the information technology field for a local company.

There were many of those days Olivia recalled over time – some that made her chuckle and others that caused a few more strands of gray hair to show themselves in the mirror. Most conversations she had with students like Sophia reminded her that the world of technology was second nature to so many. To her it was a learning journey she started as a child in Honduras. You see, Olivia was born and raised in the city of Agua Salada, just outside of the Honduran capital city of Tegucigalpa. Not only was technology a scarce resource in homes where she grew up, but it was almost non-existent. Olivia did not have a computer in her house, and her school taught nothing of how to utilize technology. Only one of her friends had a computer in his house, and that was because his father was an American expatriate who worked remotely and did business around the world.

Whenever she went out into the city, she would find reasons to visit major hotels or certain businesses that had computers or internet connectivity so she could explore the technical world that seemed in many ways to be just out of reach. Once, she met a professor visiting from Europe who was in the country to speak on the influence of technology in schools. He would be speaking at one of the area's few institutions of higher education, and being in the right place at the right time she was able to share fifteen or twenty minutes talking with him about the lack of technology at her school and changes around the world in how younger generations were using computer applications in education and at work. Olivia recalls that conversation as one of both despair and hope at the same time. She was sad to be reminded of what she did not have access to, but also hopeful of what possibilities might lie ahead for her one day. She loved everything about computers and the endless connectivity of the internet, and she knew that one day she would find her path to work in the field of information technology.

When Olivia was in eleventh grade, her aunt and uncle moved to the United States of America and with the blessing from her parents she went with them for a better chance of advancing her education in ways that still seemed just out of reach in her hometown. On the day she left home, her father told her, *"Go make a dream. Be on the lookout and when the opportunity comes along, you say yes."* After high school graduation, Olivia received a scholarship to attend a small state college. After two successful years there she transferred to a larger university and became the first person in her family to graduate with a post-secondary degree, majoring in education with a concentration in, you guessed it, technology. She taught high school computer classes at two different schools in California before moving with her aunt and uncle to Chicago, where she found a new teaching job quickly.

After a few years teaching, an opportunity presented itself to make her way respectfully out of the classroom and eagerly into the IT field. A small insurance firm was looking for an entry-level helpdesk coordinator – with an emphasis on entry-level. Olivia is pretty sure she got the job because nobody with an IT degree was willing to accept the low pay (a salary cut at the time, even for a teacher), but for her it was just the opportunity her father told her to look for, and she said yes.

The insurance company was small and had only been in business for eight months when Olivia was hired. They did not pay well, had one used coffee maker and a refurbished copy machine in the break room, none of the office furniture matched, and the computers were running on a Windows operating platform that was four years old. It was a tough road that first year, transitioning from teaching to being the one who was expected to have all the answers, but it led to hands-on experience and a return to school for multiple certifications, two promotions as the firm grew, and eventually a Master's Degree in Information Technology with a minor in network infrastructure, which the firm helped pay for. It helped that her boss, the senior partner at the insurance firm, was a genuine and kind man. He valued people and all the unique and diverse value folks brought to the table. He was a good businessman, which also meant that he knew how to treat his staff well and care for them just as he expected them to care for his company.

That startup insurance agency, the one who paid an entry-level Helpdesk Coordinator less than a teacher's salary, had grown over time to become a highly respected firm and supported & promoted Olivia to exceed her dreams. She started as a "department of one," grew to serve as the most tenured team lead in a department of three, was promoted to IT Manager for a growing team, and many years later became the Director of Information Technology leading a business unit of twenty-eight, including four new managers whom she could teach, guide, and share in their successes.

From those early discussions between teacher and student, to many conversations across her growing career in the information technology field, her professional influence has had sincere and positive impacts and Olivia has made real differences in the lives of others. Some were brief conversations teaching something new, while others were deeper and helped her people learn valuable lessons as well as useful technical and professional skills. No matter which, she always appreciated the light others shined upon her and looked for ways to being the kind of teacher, in business, who reflects that light onto others.

In the pages ahead, we will share some of these rays of light - these experiences Olivia has had - and how she applied the Adaptive Conversation Process.

# SECTION THREE:

## THE ADAPTIVE CONVERSATION PROCESS:

## *A MODEL IN PRACTICE*

# 3.0
# Every Step Matters

## STEP ONE... STEP TWO...

When you think of a process, you clearly understand that it is a series of steps laid out in succession to achieve an intended outcome. That much is clear and obvious. What may not be instinctive or even necessarily true in every process is the importance across those steps.

Think about a child on the playground. She climbs the four rails up to the monkey bars and eyes her goal – getting to the other side without falling midway. What might the high-level process be?

1) Climb the rails up to reach the bars
2) Grab the first bar with one hand
3) Lean back while maintaining your one hand grip
4) Eye the next bar
5) Swing your weight forward
6) Reach and grab for the next bar with your free hand
7) Shift your weight and repeat until you reach the end

Ok, these are basic, but it illustrates a question. Is each step in this process equally important, or perhaps even necessary? Could climbing rails either not be an option or even be needed to reach? Might leaning back be that important if the bars are close together? You get the idea. A process is important; however, not every process contains steps that are equal or even matter that much.

When it comes to the Adaptive Conversation Process, what we are saying is that each one of the five steps matters and can be seen as critical to an effective conversation.

In the section ahead, we will further explore each step, one-by-one. You will also see our friends (personas) Molly, Ezra, Carter, and Olivia. Their stories will serve as examples to further represent the importance of each step in the Adaptive Conversation Process.

# 3.1

# Step One – Clarify Purpose

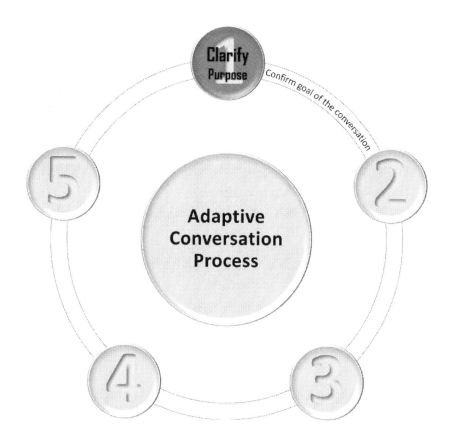

## PURPOSE DRIVES ACTION

Purpose blends deep-rooted intent with reasoning behind how or what we do enroute to reaching an outcome. One of the most valuable lessons we have learned throughout our careers is that clarity of purpose is a key driver of action.

As senior leaders across diverse industries, C-level executives at organizations from local startups to Fortune 50 companies, and managers of million- and billion-dollar P&L operations, we found that our most productive conversations always began with a clear understanding of the "why."

Whether it was setting strategic goals with a senior leader or driving performance discussions with a team member, starting with a defined purpose ensured that everyone was aligned from the outset.

For example, when leading a merger at a large corporation, the leadership team was navigating multiple complexities - from cost integration to cultural alignment. Before diving into tactical solutions, we clarified the purpose of each discussion. Whether it was to identify operational efficiencies, or to discuss integration milestones, each conversation had a specific, shared goal and being certain the purpose was fully understood by all was critical up front. This deliberate focus on purpose allowed us to move forward with precision, ultimately saving 15% on operational costs within the first year of the merger.

## WHY IS THIS SO IMPORTANT

When you are about to speak with someone, for a pre-determined reason, what is one of the first things you might think? I am sure you can answer that question in many possible ways, but I bet one of the things you might think about is how you will get your point across so the person you are speaking with understands what you are saying. This is you preparing to be clear. You are considering the approach you might take, the tone you will carry, and the words you should choose. You are reflecting on past conversations, the comprehension level of the other person, and how best to connect in the conversation for success. Being clear is important, and all your preparation from this perspective is valid and useful, though how might we also look at this from a different vantage point?

In addition to (not instead of) contemplating how best you might ensure your intent is achieved, what if we look at it from the other side. What might happen if, instead of focusing too much on asking ourselves "how can I make myself clear," we shift that focus on asking ourselves "how can I ensure the other person has the clarity needed?" What might that do for the conversation if we think first about that other person? How might that impact the rest of the conversation? This is the point of our first step in the Adaptive Conversation Process – Clarify Purpose.

We have talked with countless people over the years about conversations of all types. By far the most common sentiment was that they wished they had a magic wand to wave over the head of the person with whom they were about to have a conversation, which would somehow ensure clarity and lead their dialogue through to the best possible conclusion. Well, while we too might wish magic wands existed, beginning any conversation by clarifying purpose might just be the next best thing.

## WHAT ARE WE CLARIFYING

One of the common missteps we have seen over and over happens to be around exactly what people try to clarify in a conversation.

When entering a conversation, you already have some idea of why you are having it in the first place. If it is a teaching conversation, you know there is something the other person needs to learn and be able to do. If it is a coaching conversation, you know the other person is trying to figure out how to achieve something that may currently be a struggle or needs to change. If it is a performance conversation, you know the other person is either doing something well or, more commonly, has not met an expectation and needs to understand and take steps to improve. What often happens when we begin talking with another person is that we jump too soon into the trap of trying to clarify based on intended outcomes, whereas, what we should be focusing on is clarifying the purpose of the conversation itself before anything else.

While there is always some nuance of approach based on the type of conversation, focusing first on the purpose of why you are having the conversation and what it is meant for is consistently critical, first and foremost, across every type of conversation. Let us be clear:

First, clarify the purpose of the conversation itself...period.

## HOW TO CLARIFY

Have you ever started a conversation and then realized that the other person was not totally clear on what you were talking about, or even why you were having the conversation in the first place? Did it perhaps seem as though somehow you both were simply not on the same page? How did you know? What did they say that gave you that impression? You probably saw it in their expressions and body language and heard it in the tone of their voice. If you are at all perceptive, you can usually tell quickly if the purpose you are trying to establish is unclear. There are several things to consider as you clarify purpose.

## FRAMING

Framing is setting the stage and putting into perspective what the conversation is meant to do or address. It is the big picture, before content. If you do a good job framing the conversation, you will help focus attention on intent and immediately remove that which is outside or not relevant to the conversation at hand. It helps both you and the person with whom you are speaking to be clear up front on what the conversation is not, just as much as what it is. Framing can also preempt potential objections, resistance, or other misunderstandings depending on the type of conversation you will have. It also helps to have this frame as a point of reference; to bring the conversation back to its intended course should you veer off track.


## RECEIVER

The receiver, or person you are speaking with, is obviously important. Just as every conversation is different, every person you speak with is a unique individual with diverse experiences, needs, desires, and expectations, and they receive messages in ways that are specific to them. Remember, the other person is not you. While you may gravitate to a particular style of communication, or prefer to receive information in a certain way, and may have clarity yourself, do not assume the other person is just like you or has equal clarity. Things like professional jargon or assumptive situational knowledge that may be known by you (the sender) can derail, even momentarily, the opportunity to establish clarity of purpose. Be intentional in your understanding of the other person, their needs, and the clarity they have (or do not have), before telling yourself that the conversation can move forward.


## CONCISENESS

Being concise in a conversation is one of the things we hear a lot about as leaders, in our communication with others and especially at higher levels of leadership. It is just as important when establishing clarity of purpose in a conversation. What can be said with fewer words is usually better than what is said using extraneous references and superfluous fluff (yes, we just used those extra words on purpose to make a point). Too much complexity can create confusion, and risks clarity. We often feel like we need to over-explain things or add extra context. This usually comes from forgetting to listen more than we speak, which leads to feeling like you want to add more of your own thoughts, or intentions, or trying to lead the conversation in a certain direction from the start. Depending on the type of conversation, you may or may not need to point the dialogue in a direction, which is fine; however, over-doing it can cause the other person to create a story in their mind on what they think the conversation is about, before validating its true purpose.

## EXPECTATIONS

Expectations in a conversation are the beliefs, held by both parties, for what will happen in the engagement. They are probably the first thing the other person thinks about even before you get together or start talking. Right from the start, the other person is intently listening to determine the degree to which their expectations for the conversation will be met. The best advice here is to not make people guess. Be straightforward, transparent, and distinct so expectations can either be validated, or adjusted to then be met openly and in good faith. Be complete with how you clarify purpose, without over-engineering to intentionally leave something out for later. We often do that in conversation. We say one thing, gaining clarity, but hold something back and then introduce it to the conversation later. When we do that, it can throw the other person off and cause them to question what they thought was clear from the start. Then they start assuming, and that is not good.

Wherever there is lack of clarity and/or information deficiency, human nature fills that void with negative assumption. Avoid this through completeness of clarity for the conversation up front.

## A BIT ABOUT FOCUS

Let us preface by saying there is no singular correct thing to say, which leads to perfect clarity (again with the wish for the magic wand). What is more important is being prepared to clarify the purpose of the conversation, and then being focused on listening to ensure it exists before moving forward with additional dialogue. We have already established that doing so risks the conversation drifting back and forth, spinning off track, and ultimately being less effective than intended. Focus helps us achieve this first step in the process...so what must we focus on?

Our focus begins before the conversation does, in our preparation. When getting ourselves ready for a conversation, metacognition comes into play. This is about being intentionally aware of our own thought processes, in this case how we are thinking about the conversation to be had. Focus on what specifically is leading you to say, or ask, something as you begin. Are you thinking about why you want to say something? Are you thinking about how you want the other person to hear it? Are the words in your head clearer to you than they may be to the other person? Are you even certain about the purpose of the conversation yourself? Focusing internally, especially before the conversation, helps you be ready to establish clarity when you are with the other person.

Once in the conversation, you have a much better probability of clarifying purpose through active listening. We have all been told, especially as leaders, how important this skill is. This is more than just keeping your ears open to what is being said. Sure, that is important, especially to compare what you are hearing to what you have prepared for; however, gaining clarity requires much more. You must assign intentional focus early in the conversation on what the other person seems to be feeling and thinking, as well as how they are saying something or answering your questions.

These are the idiosyncrasies of effective communication and are paramount to establishing clarity. The purpose of the conversation can be acute, and by not allocating enough focus to active listening you might either miss that acuity or inadvertently broaden the dialogue, resulting in a less-than-optimal conversational outcome.

Establish specificity and get verbal confirmation that you are both on the same page when it comes to the purpose of the conversation before starting down a path to farther-reaching impacts or outcomes. Remember, clarifying the purpose of the conversation is the "why" for talking, and focuses on a specific thing, at a specific time, in that specific conversation. It is not really about an end-goal or final-outcome beyond your dialogue right then and there. Sure, there is almost always something down the line you are both addressing and will look for; however, focusing in the moment on the specificity of the conversation will help you to remain where you both need to be with each other, in that moment.

In gaining confirmation, leaders often mirror (repeat back) what they have heard or just said, and at a minimum ask the other if the purpose of the conversation is in fact clear.

**Let's visit with one of our four personas now**, to help illustrate the importance of using the Adaptive Conversation Process. As you read on, reflect on whether this reminds you of a situation you may have faced, or might face in the future. Make connections so you can see the need for the Adaptive Conversation Process, as well as how and when it can be helpful for you in your future interactions.

## MOLLY

Seven months before her fiftieth birthday, Molly became the Vice President of Lending for her community-based credit union, and while her success story is surely inspiring, her journey to becoming an admired leader was not without challenges and learning opportunities early on. Upon entering the banking industry, and up to when she got the nod for her most recent promotion to the senior leader role, Molly held seven different positions and amassed twenty years of experience. Although she had become something of a subject matter expert in lending, only the last seven years before her big promotion were spent as the Manager – her only meaningful role directly leading people.

Like many new leaders, at the time she became a manager Molly thought she had it all under control. She knew her stuff, she had done every function in the lending department, and she had worked with most of the team for the last twelve years. What she did not "bank on" (pun intended) was that as a people leader the conversations she would have, and particularly the coaching role she would have to play, was a brand-new experience and would become the most important development challenge she would take on.

Molly recalls one of her first real coaching conversations, which in her words she "failed miserably at." Michelle, one of her newly hired loan processors, seemed to be having a hard time connecting to the job. She progressed through their formal onboarding program, was observed and evaluated on the most common processes, and even went through their team's new "buddy system" with an experienced team member, but she was having a hard time afterwards on her own. Molly had standing team meetings every week, but that did not seem to be enough to help Michelle deal with what she was feeling. She held regular one-on-one meetings with each person on the team, but that too was not doing the trick for this new struggling team member. Something had to give. One Friday afternoon, Michelle knocked on Molly's door and came right out saying, "I need your coaching if I am to connect and succeed."

For a month and a half Molly and Michelle met every other week for "coaching." It was not part of the team meeting, or combined with her one-on-one sessions; rather, these sessions were separately scheduled and prioritized on the calendar above all else. They never canceled, and started and ended on time, hallmarks of good coaching. The problem was not their scheduling or intentions; rather, it was Molly's execution at the most basic stage in the conversation – they never really achieved clarity at the start of a session.

Sure, it was mutually understood that Michelle needed help, but that is about as clear as they ever really got before Molly would jump in with questions, suggestions, and tips for how to do the job. She would refer to something she had observed and then get right into questions like, "what did you try in that situation?" and then would jump to "have you tried this?" and "why did you do that?" Then she would proceed to retrain her in a new process, one week after another, always finding the conversation spinning around recent issues.

By the end of each conversation, Michelle left the office smiling as she would better understand how to do the specific thing they were talking about at the time, and Molly would be smiling because she would believe that progress had been made. In some ways, it had been – from a training perspective not coaching. When they would meet again, at the beginning of the next session they would look at each other and wonder what happened because, outside of that singular process that was essentially "retrained," they really made no other progress, especially in how Michelle was feeling holistically about her ability to be truly successful in the role. Rinse and repeat. It only took them five failed coaching sessions before Michelle posted internally for a different job in another department.

What went wrong? Why did these coaching sessions, which were always made a priority, fail? More importantly, how could Molly and Michelle leave their time together smiling if the sessions were not working, and how could Molly believe things were going so well when in fact they were not?

Molly reached out to one of her peers at the credit union with whom she had formed a good relationship. Her name was Carita, and she had also been with the credit union for a long time, having also been promoted from within. Molly asked what she thought, and it all became clear when Carita asked two important questions: "When you would meet, what would Michelle say she needed coaching on?" and "How would you both know what you were focusing on for that session?" Molly was speechless. She knew her mistake right away.

Each coaching session was doomed from the start because they never properly clarified the purpose of the session. It was not enough to get an affirmative head nod around something she suggested they cover based on her observations, even if there was something beneficial to be learned. Molly realized that each time they met she seemed to be the one who would identify where the conversation, and the focus, should be placed – and then tutelage would begin. Not only was she teaching rather than coaching much of the time, but she never really asked Michelle what she wanted to be coached on, to begin a session, or what she hoped to accomplish from that specific conversation. Michelle wanted to find a connection to the work beyond the "how to" parts of the job, yet Molly assumed that connection would automatically surface through deeper learning and achievement. Had clarity of purpose preceded their dialogue each session, a more appropriate direction may have been taken, which could very well have led to a different outcome for them both. They never had a chance.

## WHAT CAN WE LEARN FROM MOLLY?

What Molly took away from this experience was invaluable. At the very beginning of any coaching conversation, it is critical to ask what the goal of the specific session is to clarify purpose. This ensures both coach and coachee are on the same page. Molly never did this. Imagine leaving your house for an evening bicycle ride with your significant other, without confirming first where you are headed? You would get to the end of the driveway and quite possibly turn in opposite directions. If you do not begin the conversation by intentionally clarifying purpose, then you run the risk of never arriving at your intended destination…at least not together.

Crucial as well, true coaching should be driven by the employee – not the leader. In her conversations, Molly inadvertently set the agenda. She never asked or clarified where Michelle wanted to take their conversation and what was driving that. She instead tended to identify a problem herself as she steered the conversation and directed what needed to be done next. It is obvious that coaching was not the conversation being had, and that the intended purpose of their conversations was held to be something different by each of them, which doomed their coaching from the start.

## QUESTIONS TO REFLECT ON

How might Molly have approached coaching conversations differently?

What could Molly have asked Michelle to ensure they were on the same page and had the same understanding of coaching?

What are some things Molly could have asked to validate whether clarity of purpose had been achieved?

What might Molly have done had she realized she and Michelle were not mutually clear on their conversation's purpose?

How might Molly have shifted her approach to get a better result for Michelle?

# 3.2

# Step Two – Call Out
# The Situation

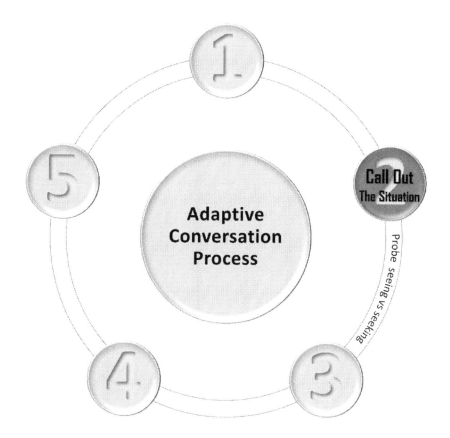

## THE CRITICAL CURRENT STATE

In every challenging environment, let alone in every conversation, a firm understanding of the current state is critical. Across our unique and diverse experiences in executive roles, we have found consistently that first openly identifying what is happening (at the time), versus what is or has been expected (later or all along), has been the primary focus in the "Call Out the Situation" step, as we see in the Adaptive Conversation Process.

For example, this approach proved to be particularly effective when we provided guidance for a division at a healthcare company that was facing underperformance in key regions. Instead of making assumptions as we engaged in several important conversations, we gathered the leadership team to methodically identify, confirm, and evaluate the current situation before expanding dialogue any further. During these conversations, we pinpointed specific inefficiencies in the supply chain and service delivery that were not immediately visible. By drawing these issues out candidly and up front, we were able to move important conversations along to identify quick-wins and long-term solutions, resulting in a 20% improvement in service levels and a stronger market position.

## VULNERABILITY LEADS TO OPEN CONVERSATION

As leaders, we have been told time and again how important vulnerability is to our growth and success with individuals and teams. There are countless authors who share their perspectives of when it makes most sense to be vulnerable, how to go about it, and why it can make such a difference. It is the same for leaders and non-leaders alike, as it does not take a title or a position of power to be more open.

Have you ever been in a conversation with one of your team members — it could have been for coaching, or mentoring, or training, or performance, or something else — and felt like you were hitting a brick wall in the discussion? I am guessing you are nodding in agreement, as we have all been there. What happened? Certainly, it could have been due to a variety of reasons; however, often if we step back and look at the conversation from the outside-in we see that someone is just not being vulnerable enough to be open to other perspectives, feedback, ideas, or probing questions. This atmosphere of being closed can stifle good conversation, no matter what kind we are talking about. This is why vulnerability is such an important precursor to having open conversations and calling out the situation with candor and transparency.

## HOW CAN WE ENCOURAGE VULNERABILITY

Sometimes shutting down fear and pushing ahead gets the job done. Other times, embracing that fear provides extra motivation to be brave and overcome a difficult situation. The right strategy for the moment can differ based on several variables; however, as we have learned from Brené Brown, world-renowned author, speaker, professor, and podcast host, "courage and fear are not mutually exclusive" (Brown, Dare to Lead).

We recall a time when we had just stepped away from working in conventional roles and joined the world of consulting. We were younger than many of the Chief Learning Officers and executive teams we were advising, and we were perfectly aware of the challenges this added to conversations we would have. On one morning, we were set to meet with the CEO and CHRO of a large manufacturing company to discuss leadership challenges they were facing with plant managers. Our firm was recommended to this company by an association's legal counsel, so we felt confident; however, within the first few minutes of the meeting we could see on the faces of these executives that they wondered how young consultants could possibly know more than they do about how to approach the challenges they were facing. We felt courageously confident and anxiously afraid at the same time, which was a healthy feeling that led us to do what we knew we must. It was time to get vulnerable.

As we listened to what the company was experiencing and the challenges being created, we paused in our conversation and shared the following:

*"What you are experiencing with your plant leaders must be very frustrating. Thank you for sharing so candidly. You both have been leaders with the company for a long time, and you might be wondering how we, a couple of consultants, could relate. We are young, haven't been out to your plant floor, and may not have the silver bullet for everything. What we can promise is that we hear what you are saying, we will listen to your leaders, do our best to understand what they need, and be honest with you about what we can and cannot do."*

From that point forward, everything about how these two seasoned executives interacted with us changed for the better. Their eyebrows unfurled, they sat back a bit more comfortably in their chairs, and they smiled a little more genuinely as we dug deeper into what they were seeing, seeking, and the gap we might help address. By making ourselves vulnerable and being courageous, the perceived barrier between us came down and we were able to talk openly and authentically.

Trust was the single most important variable that went through the minds of these two executives, and our vulnerability helped create a feeling that we could have an open dialogue and that they could trust that we would be honest in our ability to help. In the end, we contracted for leadership development solutions with the company, including 360-degree assessment, management training, and coaching on emotional intelligence competencies for their plant leaders, achieving results far exceeding those initially expected in that first meeting.

It is the same for you and the people you have conversations with. If there is a lack of trust, people will keep their guard up, in part or in full. Where trust is present, they will open themselves to listening, and contemplating, and asking, and answering, and considering something different from what they may have thought or felt at first. That is where the magic happens in conversation. Trust creates an environment where vulnerability can exist, and vulnerability leads to truth. Truth is at the core of calling out the situation upon which a conversation is set and opens doors to moving forward and being ready to consider possibilities.

## WHAT WE ARE "SEEING"

The current state in process management recognizes how something is presently done, very often with an intent to identify opportunities to optimize the process. It is important to acknowledge how something is happening before it is possible to adjust in ways that matter.

In product management, the current state identifies what something does, with an end game of finding ways to improve or maximize how it will deliver against expectations. It is critical to call out what the product does, compared to what it is intended to do, before making informed decisions on how it might change.

The same can be said when it comes to conversations. Across the many types of conversations leaders have (as we have referenced such as coaching, mentoring, training, performance, etc.), verbalizing the current state is an important element in getting the conversation going in the right direction if we are to achieve positive results and intended outcomes. This is what we mean in this step of calling out what we are seeing.

When coaching someone, we might find ourselves asking, "How are you approaching this currently?" If we are mentoring someone, we might similarly ask, "so I know better what to share, what is happening right now?" If we are having a difficult performance conversation, we might start by sharing more matter-of-factly and calling out, "the behavior I am observing right now is 'x,' are you seeing what

I am seeing?" or something similar. You get the point. Calling out the "current state" situation gets things out in the open and laid on the table. This is critical if the conversation is to then move into more of a discussion around what is to be changed, developed, considered, or even simply acknowledged.

## WHAT WE ARE "SEEKING"

There is always a reason why we are talking with someone. In casual dialogue, this reason may be minor; however, in more meaningful conversations like the ones we have been exploring, there is an important purpose. Knowing this gives us a reference point that guides discussion.

Think about your team members for a moment. Have any of them ever come to you and asked for your guidance to help find their way along a career path? Perhaps they asked you how to do something better on the job? Maybe they sought your experience in achieving improved results? I know, these are all conversations you have had countless times. They may be different types of conversations, but one very consistent part of them is always finding out, "what do you want today, and what is the current situation when it comes to getting it?" You had to ask because without knowing this there is no way you could advise, educate, share, or probe to help on these different paths.

If we are to fully address the situation ("what are you seeing?"), we must also include the end state ("what are you seeking?"). By bringing both into the open, space is created in the conversation to begin exploring the gap between the two.

In a coaching conversation, this might lead to probing questions such as, "what is happening right now?" and "what do you want that to look like?"

In a training conversation, this might lead to questions that get at closing a learning gap, such as "what is your knowledge or ability today?" and "how should that knowledge or ability level be different?"

In a performance conversation, this might lead to clearly laying out differences in expectations such as, "what did we get?" compared to "what did we expect?" and "what is the gap in performance delivered versus expected?"

The bottom line is that before we can move the conversation forward into ideation and possibility making, we must be clear on what "is" and what "should be." This establishes the conversation's reference point and target, upon which further dialogue will be based.

**Let's take a look an experience from another one of our personas**. Like before, try and connect this to what you may have experienced in your life, as well as how and when it can be helpful for you in your future interactions.

## CARTER

Everyone is not equally as adept at recalling pertinent experiences and sharing them in ways that are meaningful to others, but this was one of Carter's many gifts. Granted, he certainly had a life filled with experiences through his time in the United States Air Force that carried him across the world and placed him in situations most people might shy away from, but when it all came down to it, he just had a knack for storytelling and referencing something from his past in a way that made a point for someone else. This skill made him a great mentor.

A couple of years ago Lexi, a nurse in the intensive care unit at the small hospital where Carter had been working, was having a conversation with one of the physicians. In that conversation, Lexi shared that although she learned various calming and communication techniques for talking with family members of her patients, and she certainly had ample opportunities to put that learning into practice, there were still times when she felt ingenuine or times when a family's reaction would catch her off-guard. That physician recommended, as part of her individual development, that she should seek out a mentor. Lexi did that and found Carter, which turned out to be just what the doctor ordered.

Carter recalled a conversation he had with Lexi about empathy. In that conversation, Lexi had shared with him that, while her intentions were always sincere, she sometimes felt like she was repeating rote responses and therefore coming across as ingenuine or unempathetic. She asked Carter if he ever felt that way in his work, especially when he delivered difficult news to a patient or their family members, and how he dealt with it. Carter remembered that having conversations with empathy was something he was taught at an early age back in his college AFROTC program, which he then carried forward throughout his career in the military and beyond.

After clarifying the purpose of their intended conversation, which got to the heart of how Lexi was feeling and what she was looking for, Carter began to contextualize the story he would share and how he learned to approach people from a place of empathy and authentic communication.

*"I am sure it has been tough having trouble with this and feeling this way at times. That must feel frustrating and emotionally draining"* Carter told Lexi, to which she nodded thanking him very much. That is when Carter knew where he was about to take the conversation, as he called out the

situation, probing into what Lexi was seeing (and feeling), as well as what she was seeking (or wanted to be feeling).

*"Did I sound genuine?"* Carter asked. *"Was I being authentic with you just then?"*

Lexi did not know how to answer. She assumed Carter was sincere. Why wouldn't he be? Carter went on to tell Lexi that when he was wrapping up his senior year in college and getting ready to ship out on his first assignment in the Air Force, the Major over Aerospace Studies at the university told him to stop simply saying, "I'm sorry" when responding in conversation where empathy was his goal.

Carter asked Lexi several questions around how she was approaching and speaking with patients and their families in these situations currently. He asked what she would say and what she was pulling from when deciding how to communicate in these situations. He finally moved into asking more specifically about how that was making Lexi feel right then, before shifting gears to questions around what she wanted to communicate and how she wanted to feel. These critical questions helped articulate, in their conversation, what Lexi was seeing (current state) and what she was seeking (preferred change or future state), which made it possible to continue in a meaningful way.

*"What are you trying to do for someone when you empathize?"* Carter asked.

*"Well,"* replied Lexi, *"I guess ideally I'm trying to express that I acknowledge the pain, gravity or injustice of the situation, as a way of being caring and developing trust so we can continue necessary conversations from there."*

*"How does saying, 'I'm sorry' and then repeating pre-written or scripted responses from the hospital help you show that acknowledgement? Does it help you feel what it is you are seeking from these conversations?"* Carter followed.

Lexi knew it did not and didn't even need to answer out loud as her face showed the answer. The beauty in this part of the conversation is that Carter intentionally took time to create space for Lexi to share what she was experiencing based on what she was doing at that moment in time, in contrast to what she was driving for and wanted to feel in a more ideal way. By addressing "seeing" versus "seeking," Carter paved the way for the rest of their conversation.

For the next twenty minutes or so, Carter shared conversations he had with the Major of AFROTC, as well as his experiences since. The Major told him that saying, "I'm sorry" does little to acknowledge a person's feelings (the stated preference) and rather seems to be a canned response that people use when they do not truly know what to say (the reality of such a response she had been using followed by an even more scripted hospital response).

Carter went on to share that the Major asked him if he ever really wanted something so much that it hurt, but he didn't get it. Carter told Lexi the story. It was a catering busboy job that he wanted when he was in middle school. There was only one position open, and he was one of two people who applied. Carter wanted that job - he needed that job - to start saving money for a car. He had been looking for work but at fourteen years old it was not that easy to find a job that made any real money, and his parents told him that they would match whatever he saved over the next two years so he could buy a car. This job paid more than a dollar an hour above anything else he could find, and it was the best opportunity for him, but the other boy, who was already sixteen and had his own ride to work every weekend, got the job instead.

Carter paused and asked Lexi if she could imagine what the Major said to him next, to which she replied, *"I'm guessing he did not say, 'I'm sorry.'"*

*"Correct,"* Carter shared. *"He said, it's not fair and that really stinks."* Carter went on to ask Lexi what the Major accomplished in his response. The answer was that he genuinely acknowledged the feelings that Carter was experiencing and created an instant bond around the situation at hand making it possible to have additional meaningful conversation.

## WHAT CAN WE LEARN FROM CARTER?

By identifying what was occurring in the conversations Lexi was having with patients and how it was making her feel, and by contrasting that to what would ideally occur to make her feel the way she really wanted to feel, it put Lexi in a particular frame of mind. It helped her understand better and be ready to hear about Carter's experiences and then talk about the impact trying things differently might have. We need to remember when we have conversations as leaders that, while it is easy to assume the other person has a clear picture of the distinction between what they are seeing versus what they are seeking, that simply is not always the case. Taking the time to call out the situation and verbalize this can make a big difference and advance the conversation in the right way.

To shine a light on this part of their conversation, it was at this specific step in the Adaptive Conversation Process (calling out the situation) that Carter was able to move into sharing his own experience in a way that helped Lexi with what she was going through, which is what mentoring is all about. If he jumped directly into storytelling mode, without first framing the context through ensuring Lexi was clear on her current and future state, it may have made it more difficult to connect the lesson within the conversation to the stated purpose. Just as we do not want to jump to a solution in business, in conversations we must honor this step in calling out the situation. It sets the stage before moving forward and talking about options; thus, it is an essential sequenced step in the Adaptive Conversation Process.

## QUESTIONS TO REFLECT ON

What else might Carter have said to bring out what Lexi was experiencing in that moment?

How did Carter show what he was trying to get Lexi to understand, more than just telling her?

Why was it so important for Carter to ask Lexi directly how she was approaching and speaking with patients and their families?

How did Carter create space for Lexi to share what she was experiencing? What else could he have done?

How did Carter's personal stories, that were very different than what Lexi was going through, make a difference in their conversation?

What else might have helped Lexi connect Carter's shared experiences with her own?

How do you think Carter may have shifted from "seeing versus seeking" to identifying the gap?

How do visualization techniques that help paint a picture positively impact the ability to call out the situation?

# 3.3

# Step Three – Consider Possibilities

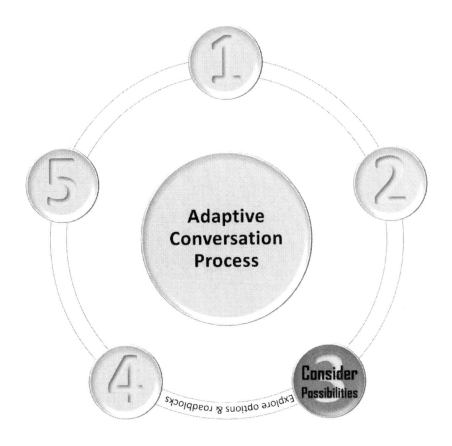

## INTO THE UNKNOWN

As seasoned leaders, we have learned through decades of experience that some of the best ideas and solutions emerge when you encourage people and teams to explore possibilities. In conversations, when the time comes to brainstorm, ideate, or consider different perspectives or possibilities, it can be easy to stray off course. This is why initially clarifying purpose and calling out the situation are so important in the process. Without these guideposts, conversations and subsequent actions may miss the mark or spin and simply waste time.

For example, when providing executive leadership for a culturally focused national non-profit professional association, we partnered with some of the largest and most well-known fortune 500 companies to improve and drive executive learning programming. Often, these clients were looking for ideas and innovative ways to build more inclusive leadership pipelines. In these cases, considering possibilities was essential for opening conversations to new, unexplored opportunities.

Instead of prescribing a one-size-fits-all solution, we engaged leaders in brainstorming multiple approaches, only after fully understanding their current state. These included examining everything from rethinking recruitment frameworks, to incorporating inclusive leadership training practices, and exploring different approaches and modalities for executive development programming.

In every case, open dialogue resulted in the development of more options, tailored methods, and actionable strategies aligned with their diversity, equity, inclusion and belonging priorities. Considering possibilities led to measurable improvements in leadership representation and engagement, far exceeding expectations. Our efforts and work continued as we led strategic planning for optimization and effective practices, but it all started with conversations.

## OPEN TO TALK ≠ OPEN-MINDED

One might assume – and they would be wrong in doing so – that just because someone is ready and willing to sit down and have a conversation that they are ready to hear what must be said. Of course, different types of conversations present a myriad of situations where readiness to hear something can differ greatly. That said, there is an element of almost any conversation that requires a level of open-mindedness, which must be confirmed. Let's dig deeper into what it means to have an open mind, and why it is so important in this step of the Adaptive Conversation Process.

## AN OPEN MIND IS A CATALYST FOR CHANGE

Have you ever had a conversation as a leader, where you knew that something was going to change, and it was your job to bring your team along successfully? What made that conversation difficult? What made things easier? We are going to go out on a limb and say that those conversations were much easier when the change was something you yourself were able to get on board with. We know that "change management" is an important part of our job; however, we would challenge that and say that "change leadership" is much more aligned as a necessary skill for people-leaders. The conversations we have with our teams can be fraught with both functional and emotional challenges when change happens, especially when it is not necessarily desirable or when it was not asked for. It is in these situations where we as leaders must challenge ourselves to have difficult conversations, not just to drive new behaviors but to, more importantly, open minds to the possibilities and new perspectives that will become a reality. Once the mind is open, space for genuine and safe contemplation can make way for the benefits of new ways to be realized.

Imposed change does not have to be the impetus for such conversations, as many types of conversations involve different changes for different reasons. In performance conversations (especially difficult ones) openness to change is usually a critical element in the dialogue. In training conversations, openness to change is important in ways that may not even be obvious, as there may be subtle inclinations to do things a certain way or subconscious predispositions that a person must be open to going against. In coaching conversations, a person has recognized a need to change in some way to achieve a stated goal, so openness to alternative ways of realizing the change is important.

What we are trying to say here is that change that is forced or imposed on a closed mind only truly affects the short-term, often leading to regression later. If open-mindedness can be achieved then there is space for authentic consideration around options, alternatives, and new ways of thinking or acting, which is where we find long-term and meaningful cognition, discussion, and lasting change.

## POSSIBILITIES AND OPTIONS

While it may seem, on the surface, that possibilities and options are the same thing, in fact they are different even though we often use the term interchangeably. When it comes to possibilities, we can look at them as being either passive (things that may or may not be able to be done), or active (things that are within our power or capacity to be done). Possibilities from a passive perspective in conversations might present themselves as "something that might happen," or "something that could happen," or "something that is able to happen." When, however, we take an active approach with possibility-making in conversations, things start to come across very differently. They present themselves as, "I could cause something to happen," or "I can ensure something happens," or "I have the power to make something happen."

What then are options, and how are they different? Like possibilities, options represent several things that we may (using active voice) cause or ensure, and that we have the power to make happen. There is an important distinction between the two though, which is that possibilities are realized in the hub space that is the open mind, whereas options require choice to make them viable. Something begins as a possibility before it may or may not become an option.

For instance, when a friend asks for possibilities on where to go for lunch, we might rattle off a dozen or more possibilities immediately; however, if that friend has certain food sensitivities or allergies, not every restaurant can accommodate those well enough for it to be considered an option.

Likewise, when we have conversations with our team members, whether for coaching, mentoring, training, performance, advice, etc. it is important to explore both possibilities and options. It reminds us of Stephen Covey's book *The 7 Habits of Highly Effective People*, where he introduces the concept of mental and physical creation. In this context, the first creation is the ideation around coming up with possibilities, and the second creation is the acknowledgement among them of options a person is willing and able to act on.

## WHAT ABOUT ROADBLOCKS?

We remember sitting through a sales training seminar many years ago. The speaker started talking about all the things that could get in the way of closing a sale. Sometimes it was a financial barrier. Other times there was something missing in what the product or service could do. Still other barriers were presented by geography or elements of fit. The fact that there were so many things that could get in the way seemed obvious, but what the speaker said was that those were almost always allowed (by the salesperson) to remain in the way by choice. That seemed odd to us. Why would someone allow an obstacle to remain in their path by choice? That is when the speaker said we must turn obstacles into objectives. We know it might sound a bit jargony, but it made sense. What he was really saying was that by looking at an obstacle as an objective, we could open our minds to possibilities for removing it, which could lead to options we could choose to act upon, which could also lead to achieving what we were aiming at in the first place.

It is the same in conversations. Once we have created a hub for possibilities and assessed them as options, we must bring obstacles into the hub so they can be dealt with.

**Let's once again touch base with one of our personas** to continue our understanding of how using the Adaptive Conversation Process gains so much. Remember as you read to think about a similar situation you may have found yourself in, or how this might apply to you in the future. Drawing parallels to conversations you will have helps you find relevance and connect to the Adaptive Conversation Process.

## OLIVIA

Olivia learned a long time ago some of the most common best practices of having performance-related conversations with team members. You know...things like:

"Take the discussion seriously."

"Move to a private and quiet place without distractions."

"Plan ahead for what needs to be communicated."

"Make it about behavior, not personal."

"Be clear."

Of course, the list goes on and over the years Olivia was very fortunate to learn about these conversations both in her formal studies and from her boss, the Senior Partner, at an insurance firm where she worked at the time.

Olivia recalled a memorable conversation she had with a team member a few years back. It was a difficult performance conversation that she was not looking forward to having at all. She had engaged in many such conversations before, but this one seemed especially difficult because expectations for a highly visible implementation were not being achieved, and the team member was typically a top performer.

The firm was making a shift to a new core processing platform, which all employees would be using in varying capacities based on their role. Janelle, one of Olivia's most trusted application and systems specialists was chosen to lead this project, largely for her prior performance and identification as a high-potential emerging leader in their talent and succession planning process. Olivia had high hopes for Janelle, which is what made this memorable performance conversation so tough.

The project itself was on schedule, but while the firm's partners expected regular updates at each stage of user acceptance testing, they tended to only hear about the project moving forward from their line of business leaders. It made them feel out of the loop, and then Olivia would hear about it from her boss at just about every interval. She knew that she could not ignore this, particularly as this was not the first conversation she had with Janelle while on the project and her goal was always to support the success of her team members. A difficult performance conversation needed to be had. It was time.

Leaning into her experience using the Adaptive Conversation Process, Olivia was quick to clarify purpose and was specific in calling out what was expected ideally compared to what was occurring. It was time to consider possibilities that might help improve performance.

If Janelle had come to Olivia and asked for coaching, the conversation's intent would have been different; however, the process and stages within would have remained the same. Since Olivia initiated this conversation to address performance challenges, the tone was more formal and the questions more direct. Olivia clearly recalled the part of the conversation where possibilities became their focus. Having revisited reporting expectations, which to be clear, were not being met, the focus of their conversation turned to getting on track just as the overall project was. Olivia asked Janelle direct questions such as:

"What seems to be getting in the way of submitting timely reports?"

"How can we explore ways to get these reports submitted as expected?"

"What might you try, which you have not yet tried, that could help?"

"What might change in your processor cadence to make this happen?"

"What do you need, which you don't have today, for you to turn this around?"

The conversation went back and forth, with Olivia listening just as much as she was talking, all the while ensuring that the tone of the conversation conveyed a sense of urgency to make changes in performance. Once Janelle shared a few possibilities that might help her get timely reporting done as expected, Olivia asked follow-up questions such as:

"How might doing that correct this expectation shortfall?"

"What leads you to believe trying this will work?"

Even in this situation, where a typically top performing team member was falling short of expectations and a difficult performance conversation was required, taking time to explore possibilities was still a critical step in an important conversation. Janelle knew the reporting expectations up front, and she knew that she was missing the mark. Olivia did not need to harp on it, but she did need to address it. By engaging Janelle in possibilities around what she needed to do to change the deficient performance, she empowered her to find and own a solution. Those possibilities then paved the way for their conversation to move through calibrating behavior change and committing to next steps.

## What can we learn from Olivia?

It was important for Olivia to help Janelle understand that feedback around the performance deficiency came from the firm's partners. By recognizing that their expectations were not being met, and by becoming aware of how they felt through only hearing about the project moving forward from their line of business leaders, Janelle was given the chance to recognize why possibilities needed to be considered.

It was important for Olivia to help contextualize and reinforce the need for possibility-making, so Janelle would not only understand why it was important, but so that she would have an innate and genuine desire to engage in the conversation.

By following the Adaptive Conversation Process, Olivia spent ample time creating space for Janelle to open her mind and come up with several possibilities for improving the performance being addressed.

When leaders know there is a performance challenge, they often already have an opinion on what the employee should do to right the ship. The easy course of action is for the leader to tell the employee what options exist, and in some situations, there may be a need to do so. The better option, in most cases, is to engage in considering possibilities together, as two people on the same side. There is little room for employee growth by just giving options, and co-creation almost always gets better results.

## QUESTONS TO REFLECT ON

How did Olivia's approach to engaging Janelle in creating possibilities help the conversation?

How did ensuring that Janelle knew expectations up front, and that she was missing the mark, add to their ability to engage openly in possibilities?

What was Olivia sure to do, immediately after Janelle offered a few possibilities to consider?

How does possibility-making in these types of conversations flex when they happen with team members who are typically top performers?

What might Olivia have said to be careful not to demotivate a team member identified as high potential for succession, and still expect earnest consideration of possibilities?

How does actively pulling obstacles into the conversation – real or perceived – further empower an employee to own the process of considering possibilities?

# 3.4

# Step Four – Calibrate Change

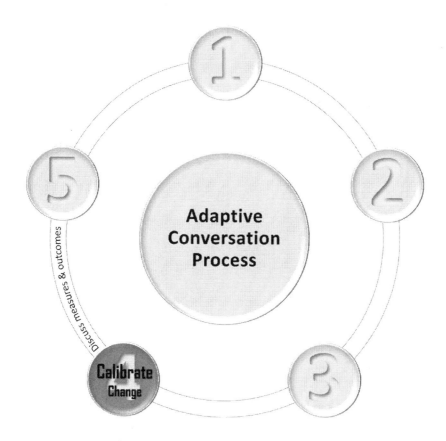

## CALIBRATION MATTERS

Calibrating change means helping gauge "the how" needed to shift behaviors or actions to achieve desired goals. This step in the Adaptive Conversation Process is critical in maintaining momentum and guiding the conversation toward measurable and impactful outcomes. It is where theory becomes practice, and intentions turn into actions that make a difference.

Think of calibrating change in a conversation like tuning a musical instrument before taking the stage for a recital.

Recognizing and making small adjustments ahead of time can create harmony and ensure that everything aligns with intended plans. In conversations, calibrating change means being clear about what needs to shift, to what degree, and why it matters. It is about ensuring that the steps toward change are actionable and realistic. It confirms the reasoning behind intended actions and ensures their expected impacts are understood.

When you are in a leadership or coaching role, for example, calibration is not about dictating change. It is about guided inquiry and the co-creation of a plan for improvement or development with another person. Asking questions that prompt examination of possible actions help gauge potential appropriateness and impact.

By calibrating change in a conversation, you help the other person map out the degree to which specific behaviors or actions may need to change and outline a plan to measure that progress.

## PAUSE FOR RELIABILITY AND VALIDITY

One of the most critical aspects in strategic leadership conversations is the ability to recognize when it is time to adapt and adjust. In the case of calibration, it is about taking a graduated view of initially confirmed or expected change and exploring, in the conversation, whether adjustment in metrics or measurement is needed.

For example, during a large-scale leadership development initiative we led for a global leader in climate solutions and sustainability services, calibrating change was a crucial part of our strategic conversations. We collaborated with highly intelligent and experienced stakeholders and found early on that their initially implemented plan was not delivering early results as expected. Recognizing this, we intentionally doubled our focus in the "Calibrate Change" step within the Adaptive Conversation Process. In doing so, we created space in our conversations to step back and take a proactive pause so that we might examine reliability (the expected consistency) and validity (the expected accuracy) of the measured change and results we sought. We were then able to flesh out and reassess metrics, finding that iterative incremental adjustments were necessary in the learning modules and assessment tools we were using.

Adding a calibration of expected change was not just about course correction (though it certainly regulated pace to ensure we were on the right track). It also involved confirming and rethinking how we measured success to better align with organizational goals. As a result, we shifted our focus to more relevant KPIs, which led to a 40% improvement in leadership competency scores within just twelve months. The commitment to calibrate change in our conversations made it possible to continuously assess and refine our approach, which proved to be the key to driving sustainable improvement.

## FOOLS RUSH IN

To this point in your conversation, you focused on clarifying purpose, called out the situation as it stands currently along with a future-focused desired state, and considered possibilities among a myriad of options as well as barriers that may require attention. All this has taken considerable effort, so why would you risk going too fast and jeopardizing the integrity of the conversation?

It might sound obvious to take your time, and this in fact is a critical aspect of the Adaptive Conversation Process – spending adequate time on each step before moving to the next. Still, even after spending significant time and effort, this is where many leaders find themselves unknowingly rushing to wrap things up too quickly. Whether it feels like you have been engaged too long, or the other person wants to move things along, or you have a hard stop in your schedule, resist the urge to jump too quickly into calibrating the change you have discussed in the conversation. When, however, you are ready for this step, enter it with the gravity and importance it deserves, as this step leads to visible outputs and tangible evidence of progress.

## MEASURE VS METRIC

Have you ever been asked, perhaps in a strategic planning session or a quarterly business review meeting, to share how you would be measuring goals or successes for your business unit, or your department, or perhaps even for an initiative? How did you answer? Were you really providing an answer about measurement, or were you sharing a metric? There is a difference.

Measurement is a quantifiable marker (usually numeric) that shows value or movement between at least two points. For example, a baseball player hits three fly balls in a single game. The first ball travels two hundred and sixty-five feet in the air before it is caught. The second fly ball travels three hundred and twelve feet in the air before it is caught. Finally, the third fly ball travels four hundred and twenty-six feet in the air, over the center field fence for a home run. The distance the ball travelled each time the batter took up his bat are all measurements. The increase in relative distance among all three hits represents metrics.

So, why is this important to understand in the context of conversations? Whether you are leading a coaching session for a manager, discussing the performance of a team member, or advising a client, there is something that led to the dialogue and is expected as an outcome. Something must be measurable for it to be intentionally controllable and for someone to be held accountable. This is reflective of what we have read about by Peter Drucker, as he proposed that we cannot manage what we cannot measure.


## CALIBRATED MEASURES MEAN MORE

You know how important measurement is, so of course this will be an important part of the conversation; however, measurement can be tricky. Imagine you are having a coaching conversation with one of your managers. Her goal was to increase the amount of discretionary effort among her team members. She decides in this conversation that for the next month she will take certain actions in how she engages with her team, giving them greater autonomy, and then gauge the increase across various work inputs and outputs.

On the surface, it sounds like a reasonable approach to measurement; however, what outside forces may or may not be at play? Is a bi-annual performance review coming up? Are any team members competing for a promotion? Has anyone you are observing in this group had a performance related conversation recently, which would impact effort to overcome potential consequences? These are all variables that could impact measures and metrics derived from the decision to give the team greater autonomy.

Taking time to plan actions that will be measured, but failing to also calibrate possible effects from variables, could shortchange the conversation. Likewise, every team member is unique and different. Without calibrating the differences (and similarities) among team members, the expected analysis of measurement could be less complete or at least not fully accurate. It is for this reason that calibration is important.

## THE FOREST FOR THE TREES

The value and importance of measurement is well known and widely accepted; however, hyper-focus within dialogue can become a landmine if we are not careful. This is another reason why calibrating change is so important to effective conversations.

You have certainly experienced something like the following across your own professional experiences:

- One of your team members has identified (or perhaps has been told or assigned) a goal - a thing to change on the road to improvement or achievement of some sort.

- You have a conversation with this team member about the varied aspects of what could, should, or must be done.

- As part of the conversation, and knowing the objective to be realized, together you pinpoint the change and even identify what will be measured.

- Then...along the way...your measure or metric somehow becomes the most important thing, above all else, and the conversation either stalls or turns into a report around percentage of achievement to goal...period.

This is a common pitfall in conversations when change is left uncalibrated. If measurement of the change becomes the hyper-focus of conversation, you risk missing a lot of good along the way and passing up opportunity for deep and fruitful conversation. You also risk the critical opportunity to pause, calibrate affects and directions, and then adjust measurement or other elements of the work based on what else may have been achieved and/or may affect your efforts.

## LEAD AND LAG MEASURES

Calibrating change in the right amounts and at the right time in a conversation is where decisions from the first three steps in the Adaptive Conversation Process start forming a predictive proof. The impact of possibilities that are to become actions can only be truly confirmed if they are fleshed out in advance, calibrated on a continuum spanning reality and potential effect, and established (and reconfirmed) as having evaluative merit. Asked plainly, how will you know actions have been taken, and intended change has occurred and/or generated outcomes as expected, immediately and ongoing?

This is where the conversation distinguishes lead measures - actions that will be taken in parts, from lag measures - the goal achieved by the sum of all lead measures. Since lag measures are often achieved slowly over time, the importance of calibrating lead measures is critical to ongoing conversations. Since change happens at an individual level, calibrating the impact of lead measures over time generates more fruitful discussion on the path to realizing the conversation's ultimate purpose. Skipping this step in the conversation process or not giving it enough attention from both a lead and lag measure perspective, creates an inefficiency as well as a risk to the change that the conversation is after.

## EXAMPLES OF CALIBRATION QUESTIONS:

- How will you know these actions are making a difference?

- What can we expect to see happen as a result?

- What needs to shift for us to achieve the outcomes discussed?

- To what degree will this shift affect the intended outcome?
- How can you tell if progress is being made on this issue?

- In what ways can we measure the impact of these actions?

- What adjustments can be made to ensure better results?

**Let's explore an experience from one of our four personas,** to help illustrate the importance of calibrating change in the Adaptive Conversation Process. As you read on, think back to a conversation, project, or initiative you were on and see if you can make any connections from your experience. Discussing measures and outcomes is a critical step in effective conversations, but doing so without calibrating change can be troublesome, as you'll see.

## EZRA

In title, Ezra served as the Director of Sales; however, at the core of his professional experience he had certifications and a background rich in project management. He excelled at leading teams through complex challenges and took pride in helping to develop solid practices that included thoughtful change management as his teams led various projects meant to grow business and increase revenue.

Ezra kicked off his new fiscal cycle with an important project that would set the tone for a strong campaign and align with the organization's multi-year enterprise strategic growth plan. Understanding the nature of sales with respect to the need for a fast start, Ezra formed a cross-functional project team with urgency, including representation from every area within the organization that had meaningful stakeholders. This included key members of his sales team, as well as leaders from marketing, information technology, product, operations, finance, learning & development, and human resources.

With this team, Ezra was able to move rapidly through initial phases of project management. He laid out a work breakdown structure that included all facets of the project, including dependencies and time-bound packages. He engaged the team to identify risks and built an assessment framework complete with initial thoughts around avoidance, mitigation, transfer, and acceptance of various risks. He established an approach for change management that considered the people-side of change, introducing checks and balances so expectations would not get ahead of awareness or readiness across his sales team. Ezra was in the zone and shared how the team would see positive effects from the tools he introduced. As the project progressed, he had everything well in-hand...or so he thought.

One morning, Ezra came into the office early and found three separate emails from different people on his project team. As he read them, it was clear that all three were saying the same things. They felt overwhelmed by the sheer formality of his project planning and needed help understanding what it all meant with respect to their roles and expected next steps. This was the first time Ezra had heard this from the team as he prided himself on good communication, yet the team seemed to be struggling.

During their next team meeting, Ezra pointed the conversation toward addressing the feelings expressed, only to find out that several others on the team felt the same way. For the next hour, Ezra used the Adaptive Conversation Process to structure a conversation so that everyone remained engaged and focused. The shifted purpose for that meeting was clarified and the situation was called out by giving everyone a voice in sharing what they were seeing, experiencing, and feeling compared to what they expected. Once the conversation made it through considering possibilities it was time to calibrate change, and this is where Ezra realized where he had fallen short in the first place.

Early actions taken included the creation of a work breakdown structure, risk assessment, and change management plan, which were meant to provide the clarity needed so that everyone could ensure they were informed and on track along the way. What Ezra failed to do in those early conversations was to calibrate whether the creation of those tools alone was enough to achieve his goal of full understanding and progress for the team. Had he spent time calibrating, he would have learned that nobody on the team had half as much experience in project management as he did, and that the complexities of some elements made things more difficult to understand and follow.

Together, they calibrated how they would gauge the degree to which these tools were helping everyone on the team. They adjusted the approach by adding actions to include some education on project management and the tools he had introduced. They also built in regular touchpoints to ensure continued understanding of each tool along the way. This helped effectively gauge that giving time to learn the tools would yield the expected outcomes of their existence in the first place. These were meetings separate from regular project update meetings, to ensure they only focused on measuring understanding and the supportive nature of the tools. Finally, they implemented a project team buddy system, wherein those who understood the tools more would help others who were not as comfortable with them.

By spending time calibrating how the team would know they understood what these tools were telling them, and could use them effectively, everyone was able to fully engage as initially expected. In this case, calibration was not just measuring the impact of the tools themselves. It was about dedicating energy in their conversation around how they would know that the tools were understood rather than assuming engagement and expected impact. Discussing measures while calibrating change was important, but acknowledging the team's lack of understanding and exposure to them in the first place was a roadblock which, left uncalibrated initially, created the team's challenge in the first place.

## WHAT CAN WE LEARN FROM EZRA

Ezra is a seasoned professional – a director level leader. He has next-level certifications and a background in project management. He had been there, done that, and knew exactly what he wanted to do. Is there a chance that he got a bit too excited to show his expertise, or to utilize the depth of knowledge he gained? Quite possibly, yes.

As seasoned leaders, we must take a breath especially when we have deep or extensive experience with something we want to utilize. Ezra has obvious project management acumen; and knew what he needed to put in place to manage the project successfully. Unfortunately, he sped right by most others on the project. By leaving them behind, the measure of success he expected by implementing project management tools was not able to be achieved. This is the beauty of calibrating change. It is not only about determining to what degree measures may be accurate or appropriate, but also whether the measures themselves are ready to be put in place.

## QUESTIONS TO REFLECT ON

How might assumption adversely affect our ability to measure impact as expected?

How could unconscious beliefs that are previously held impact measurement?

In what ways does engaging the team in calibrating change align with critical tenets of change management?

What is the difference between measures and outcomes, and why is recognizing this important?

How do we know what needs to be measured and what does not, and how should each be approached in the conversation?

How might calibrating change impact the various possibilities generated in the prior step in the conversation?

# 3.5
# Step Five – Commit to Act

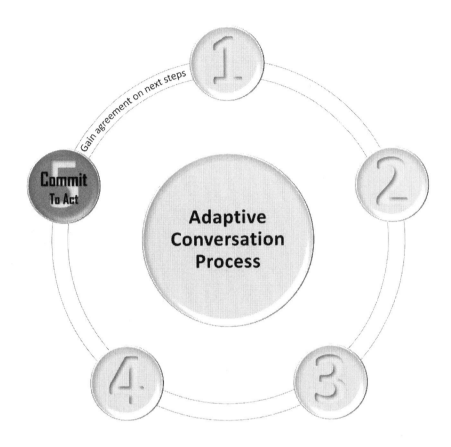

## COMMITMENT MATTERS

Without commitment, conversations and any expectation of what will follow remains theoretical. The "Commit to Act" step in the Adaptive Conversation Process is about transforming the purpose, situation, possibilities, and calibrations discussed into clear, actionable steps. By the end of a conversation, both parties should know precisely what is expected, what will be done, and when progress will be revisited. This step ensures accountability and sets the stage for future success.

During this step in the conversation, as a leader you must ensure that the other person is fully onboard with the next steps and feels confident in executing them. It is one thing to hear the other person say what will be done, but it is altogether different to ensure they are with you in that moment and ready to move from talk to action. Commitment should be specific and stated in the simplest terms. It should be measurable in consideration of the calibration discussion, and there should be clear timeframes around when something will happen - who will do what and by when.

Verbal (and, if appropriate, written) confirmation of agreed-upon actions is critical at this stage. This ensures that the conversation ends with both parties having a shared understanding of what will happen next.

Note too that once someone has committed to act, it is important to revisit the conversation and track progress against that commitment. Following up ensures the conversation was not just a formality, but a catalyst for real change.


## LEAVE NOTHING TO CHANCE

Without clear action steps, even the best dialogue may not lead to real change. By this stage in a conversation, you have discussed some significant viewpoints, reflective acknowledgements, and tangible possibilities regardless of the type of conversation; however, all that conversational progress stands to be lost if a commitment to something equally as tangible is not made. We have seen firsthand how important it is to turn insights and revelations from conversations into concrete action, by confirming a commitment to act.

One example comes from work we did with a major healthcare provider, where we helped develop a leadership diversity strategy. A strong commitment to act was critical, to say the least. After conducting a deep organizational assessment, we knew initial debriefs would fall short of meaningful action, so we moved well beyond explanations and recommendations. We worked intimately with executive leadership and cross-functionally with stakeholders to calibrate and then ensure commitment to actionable steps in distinct terms. These included setting unique representation targets, expanding cross-boundary mentorship programs, and building a proper talent pipeline from underrepresented communities.

By ensuring our client finalized, verbalized, and committed to executing these commitments, we were able to close an important loop in our conversations. This led to successful actions that aligned with measurable and tracked accomplishments. The client saw a 15% increase in leadership diversity within a year, a testament to the power of accountability and one which could have just as easily been left to chance if not for a firm commitment to act.

## WHAT IS NEXT?

Have you ever had a conversation that just assumed what was next? It is not uncommon for leaders to feel as though a conversation has clearly concluded so asking "what is next" feels a bit redundant. Depending on the type of conversation, and how the dialogue has gone, that may be true; however, it does not make it any less important.

You and the other person have spent a great amount of energy in the conversation and, much like a good article or story, you both need a firm closing to bring it all together. When a conversation closes with assumptions on what will happen next, there is no assurance that anything will happen at all. Where ambiguity exists, expectations may be misinterpreted, misprioritized, misaligned, and simply mistaken.

When the next steps are misinterpreted, actions to follow may not be taken as expected, which could just as easily render the conversation useless. Sometimes this occurs when expectations are not explained or expressed in clear enough terms. It is possible to clarify purpose up front well enough and still lack clarity in the expected next steps.

When the next steps are misprioritized, actions to follow may be assigned an incorrect level of importance. This can lead to more significant actions being neglected in favor of other actions.

When the next steps are misaligned, actions to follow may diverge from the intended path or purpose of the conversation. They might feel right, or even be valuable depending; however, if not aligned to whatever the goal of the conversation was, they risk falling short of achieving intended outcomes.

When the next steps are mistaken (by either party in a conversation) nobody wins. This is perhaps the most critical reason for clarifying what exactly the next steps will be. This does not mean every detail needs to be drawn out; however, it does call for ample energy to be applied in ensuring everyone is on the same page, and actions that follow the conversation were accurately conceived are correctly understood by all.


## COMMITMENT COMES AFTER CLARITY

Leaders certainly gain a measure of confidence at the end of a conversation when the other person can clearly and correctly verbalize the next steps regardless of the type of conversation.

In a coaching conversation, a coachee may state what will be tried next as experimentation for growth continues.

In a performance conversation, a team member may reiterate specific steps to be taken to remediate or correct behavior.

In a teaching conversation, a trainee may state positively what steps will be taken next to gain success or achievement.

Verbalizing and acknowledging what will be done next is important; however, just as important is the commitment to make good on those actions.

Commitment is the thing that moves effort from being an externalized plan to becoming an internalized promise. You might ask, how can a leader have any control over the internalization of commitment by another? That is a good question, and on some level, we would agree – you cannot. In the end, you do not have control over someone else's commitment; however, as a leader you can encourage, embolden, and energize someone to act. One of the best ways to do this is within this step of the Adaptive Conversation Process. By taking time as a leader to commit to this step, you are modeling the importance of commitment necessary to move the conversation from talk to action.

Commitment is more than one person in a conversation saying what will be done, it is an agreement and deep promise of what will follow even in the face of difficulty, pressure, or potential obstacles. Conversations begin with clarity of purpose for a reason, and they must close with commitment to act in support of that purpose.

# A NOTE ABOUT ACCOUNTABILITY

As we have acknowledged, you cannot truly control someone else's commitment, yet leaders can use this step in the Adaptive Conversation Process to cultivate ownership. In other words, by reserving time and energy to gain agreement on next steps in a way that embraces the need for commitment, the discussion around accountability can become a launching pad for self-directed action.

From what we have read in Korn Ferry's research and what we have seen within the global norms and performance correlations in their Leadership Architect, ensuring accountability seems to be one of those competencies correlated with high performance – from the individual contributor level as well as up through the front line, mid-level, business unit, and even senior executive levels of leadership. It is also one of those competencies that has all too often become an organizational buzz word with little concrete guidance on what it really is or how to find your way toward more of it. Accountability is part and parcel to this final step in the Adaptive Conversation Process.

Accountability is not just doing what you say you will do. That is closer to how we would define integrity. Accountability is not just doing what you are supposed to do. That's closer to how we define responsibility.

So…what is accountability?

That question led to the building of this model. It represents four quadrants along axes of "external expectation" and "internal commitment."

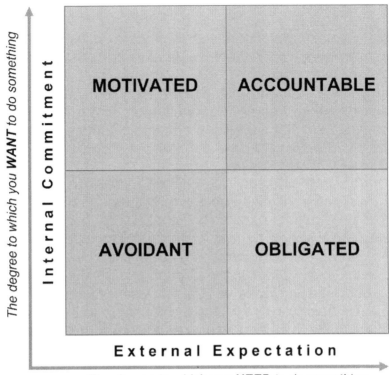

The degree to which you **WANT** to do something

Internal Commitment

| MOTIVATED | ACCOUNTABLE |
| AVOIDANT | OBLIGATED |

External Expectation

*The degree to which you NEED to do something*

If gaining a commitment to act is the leader's goal in wrapping up the conversation, then being accountable to that commitment is the goal of the other party in the conversation.

As the model indicates, where there is both a high-level of external expectation and a high level of internal commitment, you will find accountability. As the leader, depending on the type of conversation you are having, you may be setting, asking, explaining, sharing, or even advising with respect to external expectation. By taking time in the "Commit to Act" step of the Adaptive Conversation Process, you are helping the other person to internalize their commitment and therefore increasing the likelihood of accountability.

**EXAMPLES OF COMMIT TO ACT QUESTIONS:**

- What are the next steps you will take?

- When will you begin? What starts tomorrow?

- Is this something you can commit to, right now?

- On a scale of 1-10, how important are these next steps to you?

- What do you need to take these actions?

- When will we check back in to review how things are going?

**Let's look once again at an experience from one of our personas,** with respect to verbalizing expected actions as a critical closing to effective conversations. Think about conversations you have had with your team members, or even conversations you may have had with your leader. Try and connect this with how you have wrapped up conversations, both in terms of confirmation as well as - importantly - commitment.

## EZRA

Six weeks before mid-year performance check-ins with his team members, Ezra determined that it was necessary to have a difficult performance-related conversation with Mikaela, one of his more experienced sales representatives. Over the years, Mikaela had consistently performed satisfactorily, never really failing to achieve expectations but also never particularly exceeding them either. To begin the new year, Ezra and the team agreed to put a couple important processes in place, which would help grow sales and relationships as well as encourage efficiency in tracking and shared communication.

As the prior year was concluding, Ezra took time with the team to meet extensively for communication and training on two important processes they would implement immediately as of January first. These included updating every active prospect's status and/or notes in the CRM at least once every other week, as well as contacting every active client by phone at least once every other month. While everyone on the team was doing a great job keeping up on this, Mikaela was an outlier and was consistently not meeting this expectation.

By the middle of February, Ezra spoke briefly with Mikaela about this. Six weeks later, during their informal quarterly check-in meeting, he addressed this again. Since Mikaela was something of a veteran on the team, who had been consistent in prior years, Ezra again asked Mikaela to follow these processes and right after their meeting he saw activity; however, that only lasted a couple weeks. Ezra knew that another performance conversation would need to be more formal and had to make a difference. For this reason, Ezra used the Adaptive Conversation Process to guide a more effective one-on-one meeting.

Ezra set the tone up front, so that Mikaela would know the conversation was going to be serious. As a matter of fact, Ezra shared the Adaptive Conversation Process with Mikaela, letting her know that since they would have a difficult performance conversation, he was going to ensure they engaged in a structured manner, together. He clarified the purpose of their conversation in no uncertain terms up front. He shared what he saw happening with respect to not following processes, compared to expectations, and gained agreement on the gap that existed. They spent some time considering the possibilities of how Mikaela could get past any barriers she was feeling, without allowing it to become a debate. Once they identified how she might fix this issue, and they calibrated how they would know that she was on the right track, Ezra paused in a serious yet supportive tone and asked Mikaela for a commitment to act. This final step in the Adaptive Conversation Process was critical in this difficult performance conversation.

They set specific and measurable next steps to help Mikaela follow the processes, as well as steps Ezra would take to help remove obstacles Mikaela shared as potentially getting in her way. Ezra closed their conversation, in this final step of the Adaptive Conversation Process, as follows:

*"In this conversation you said, out loud, the next steps you will take. I have documented what you said, as well as what I have agreed to do for support. Can you commit to taking these steps? Can you commit to the process ongoing? As agreed, by the mid-year performance review I will see an above-average uptick in your CRM updates and client phone calls to catch up. Throughout the second half of the year, you will meet CRM updates and phone contact measures outlined in our process 100%. If I do not see this, I will follow up with you right away, at which time we will set a performance improvement plan with additional time-bound expectations and/or consequences. Does this work for you? Do you have any other questions?"*

It was important for Mikaela to first verbalize the steps she would take, rather than simply having Ezra state them, which he reiterated for added clarity. By saying them out loud, she was grounding ownership in her words, as opposed to just nodding in compliance. It was equally important for Ezra to ensure Mikaela was committed to act and meet expectations. By addressing the element of commitment separate from the actions alone, Ezra helped Mikaela internalize the weight of what she was accountable for.

The next six weeks went by quickly until it was time for the mid-year review, at which time Ezra and Mikaela revisited their agreement. At the end of the year, when it was time for Mikaela to write her self-evaluation in advance of annual reviews, it was clear to her that their conversation made a big difference. She met expectations in the process every month and saw an uptick in the contracts she closed by following it. Additionally, the sales team's client satisfaction survey proved what she already felt inside, which was that her client relationships were stronger than they had been in a long time. Mikaela wrote in her self-evaluation that she could not have achieved the results she was seeing without that very specific performance conversation with Ezra. By communicating in a very structured manner, using the Adaptive Conversation Process, and by doubling down on her commitment to act, a successful way forward was made possible.

## WHAT CAN WE LEARN FROM EZRA

Difficult performance conversations can be among the most challenging, which is often why leaders either avoid them or do a mediocre job at having them. This does not have to be the case. In his conversation, Ezra started off on the right foot by setting a serious yet supportive tone. In fact, he made a strategic choice by choosing to share the Adaptive Conversation Process with Mikaela up front. Just because you are a leader, does not mean that you stop learning along the way. By sharing that he was going to use the Adaptive Conversation Process, something he had learned, Ezra was humanizing himself, making himself vulnerable just as he would be asking Mikaela to do, and this helped prepare for a productive performance conversation.

Once decisions were made as far as what Mikaela would do, Ezra was very straightforward in asking for commitment. They set specific and measurable next steps, but it was important for Ezra to get a verbal commitment from Mikaela. That might seem small, but it was important. He also showed his commitment to the actions agreed upon, which would help remove obstacles Mikaela shared as potentially getting in her way. This is a great way to gain commitment by also showing it in equal measure,

Finally, we saw Ezra set timebound markers for action, one by the mid-year performance review and another throughout the second half of the year. This ensured specific actions and measures, but also differentiated the commitment that was expected, and made it clear as the final element in the conversation.

## QUESTIONS TO REFLECT ON

What makes differentiating stated next steps and commitment to them critical in closing a conversation?

How might you gauge the level of commitment while in the conversation? What about later?

How can you ensure a commitment to act aligns with the measures discussed?

How might you respond if a commitment to act is not as forthcoming as you would expect?

What might you do if a shift in action is necessary based on the level of commitment you are hearing?

What does expressing shared commitment do to strengthen relationships and enable stronger conversations?

# SECTION FOUR:

## THE ADAPTIVE CONVERSATION PROCESS:

## *TOOLBOX*

# 4.0
# Models & The Adaptive Conversation Process

## THIS AND THAT...NOT OR

The beauty of the Adaptive Conversation Process is the ease in how, based on the conversation at hand, it serves as a single framework that can be adapted to any type of conversation.

By following the steps of this conversation process, less time and effort is wasted moving from one model to another, and more energy can be focused on the conversation at hand. It is flexible and inclusive of techniques leaders may have learned across their diverse development, while serving the expectation leaders have for pragmatic simplicity.

We know that leaders want something they can use that works well in practice and not just in theory, and that is precisely why the Adaptive Conversation Process is so great. It is a practical tool that is straightforward and immediately beneficial.

So...what does that mean for all those other models that have been published and used for centuries?

They still exist. They are still valid. They are still worthwhile, and leaders are still encouraged to utilize them as the situation and their preferences dictate.

So then, how is this done?

The answer is evident in one word – integration. By integrating the tenets of any model appropriate to the situation, one can still adhere to its purpose and intent, while allowing the Adaptive Conversation Process to guide dialogue along a path that makes sense and avoids drift.

## THE ADAPTIVE CONVERSATION PROCESS:
## AN INCLUSIVE MODEL

The Adaptive Conversation Process shows how truly inclusive it is, as it leaves open the ability for leaders to adhere to the tenets of models that may have guided and served them well in the past, while delivering value in process, simplicity, and above all adaptability.

We will explore this in the pages ahead as we look at a few of the most common conversations leaders have, and the models they often use.

While leaders have many kinds of conversations, we will focus on the most common herein, and a few frequently referenced models or approaches used in coaching, mentoring, teaching, and performance.

## INTEGRATING THE ADAPTIVE CONVERSATION PROCESS WITH COMMON COACHING MODELS

There are many more coaching models than we will take time to cover in these pages; however, it makes sense to mention just a few of those we see frequently in use.

By acknowledging them, and understanding them, we can still respect their tenets while following the practical steps in the Adaptive Conversation Process. We can keep all we have learned from these and other approaches to coaching while recognizing, though integration, the value and strength that the Adaptive Conversation Process offers.

Let's look at a few common approaches to coaching you may have seen before:

### GROW

The GROW model, developed by Sir John Whitmore, is quite possibly the one we have seen most often. It has been used by many leaders and coaching practitioners largely due to the simplicity of its four parts, which are:

**G**oal       What is the person is trying to achieve?

**R**eality      What current situation is the person in?

**O**ptions     What might be tried to achieve the goal?

**W**ill       What will the person commit to do?

The GROW acronym is clever and easy to remember, which is likely a contributing factor in why we see it referenced so often. Leaders who resonate with it can still integrate its tenets in dialogue as they utilize the Adaptive Conversation Process.

**Goal:**

This is what the person is trying to achieve. It is the thing to be changed or improved that the coachee has in mind when asking for coaching.

**In the Adaptive Conversation Process**, this is essentially the very first thing addressed. Through inquiry, the coach will **clarify the purpose** of the conversation, confirming both the intent of the session and the goal as described by the coachee.

**Reality**:

This represents the current state. It is the truth about what the coachee is facing and wants to impact though coaching.

**In the Adaptive Conversation Process**, this is fleshed out in the step where we **call out the situation**. Through open-ended probing, we discover what the coachee is "seeing" currently. This step in the process takes dialogue even further, as it critically calls out and compares what the coachee is "seeking" as an alternate (or better) outcome in achieving the goal.

**Options**:

This is searching for new ways to achieve the goal. It represents doing something different from that which produced the current reality.

**In the Adaptive Conversation Process**, this is a crucial step where coach and coachee **consider possibilities** and **calibrate change**. It is here, in this meaty part of the conversation, where we might explore alternative options, acknowledge roadblocks, and discuss measures that would indicate successful outcomes that achieve the goal.

**Will**:

This is what the person will do following the coaching session.

**In the Adaptive Conversation Process**, this is discussed in the final step, where the coachee will **commit to act**. Here, an agreement has been made for next steps, a go-forward plan has been hatched, and (importantly) a genuine commitment has been confirmed.

## OSCAR

OSCAR is another popular approach used in coaching.

Originally described by Karen Whittleworth and Andrew Gilbert, it is common among academics and practitioners and has been referenced by those teaching others basic foundations. As the acronym suggests, it has five parts, which are:

**O**utcome      What is the outcome the person desires?

**S**ituation     What does the person acknowledge as current?

**C**hoices     What choices might be made toward the outcome?

**A**ctions     What strengths can be tapped to act?

**R**eview     What has been discussed that leads to next steps?

The OSCAR model is outcome focused. Leaders who appreciate these tenets could easily integrate them in dialogue using the Adaptive Conversation Process.

## Outcome:

This is what a person desires as a result, or an outcome.

**In the Adaptive Conversation Process**, this is confirmed up front as the coach will first **clarify purpose**, initially clearly acknowledging the purpose of the conversation itself, and then confirming the goal that is desired, which aligns with this tenet.

## Situation:

This is what the person acknowledges as currently happening, which has led to the need for coaching.

**In the Adaptive Conversation Process** this part aligns well, as the coach will **call out the situation**, asking questions about what the coachee is currently seeing happening. Dialogue continues at a deeper level in this step of the process to additionally confirm what the coachee seeks that is different from the current situation, adding greater clarity to the gap that exists.

## Choices:

This is what the coachee might choose to do in moving toward a desired outcome.

**In the Adaptive Conversation Process** this too aligns well, as the coach encourages and probes for the coachee to **consider possibilities**. Generating possible options is important, as it precedes the choice to try something this model suggests. This step in the process also commits time to identifying roadblocks, which helps inform choice. It further explores what they could mean and what might be done proactively to deal with barriers.

### Actions:

These are actions or improvements that may be made, and the strengths the coachee might tap into when taking them.

**In the Adaptive Conversation Process**, this is when possibilities that have been considered become options the coachee may choose to act upon. These actions are then examined with measurement in mind to **calibrate change**. The coachee articulates how certain actions would impact goal achievement and the degree to which those actions would indicate growth.

### Review:

This is what has been discussed around next steps and how coach and coachee will follow-up with each other.

**In the Adaptive Conversation Process**, the coachee is encouraged to verbalize the next steps to confirm what will happen going forward, and to cement ownership. This step in the process takes dialogue a step further as **commitment to act** is recognized as critical to closing an effective conversation.

## CLEAR

The CLEAR model, formulated in the early 1980s by Peter Hawkins, focuses on transformational change as opposed to single-goal attainment. It can be useful, as the acronym suggests, in showing how coach and coachee will engage, while keeping track of ongoing reference points along a path of intended transformation. This approach contains five stages of engaging in coaching, which are:

**C**ontracting — What are the expectations of coach and coachee?

**L**istening — What will the coach do in listening actively?

**E**xploring — What options and perspectives exist?

**A**ction — What steps must be taken next?

**R**eview — What is the progress toward transformation?

The CLEAR model is rarely used for one-off coaching conversations, as it is more of a longer-term approach for coaching. Still, the stages in this model are sound, and valuable, so leaders who follow these tenets could integrate them into dialogue using the Adaptive Conversation Process.

## Contracting:

These are expectations that are set between coach and coachee. They establish an agreement.

**In the Adaptive Conversation Process** this is part of the step when the coach will **clarify purpose**. The intent of the conversation, for those ascribing to the CLEAR model, will be long-term. Regardless of duration, the purpose of the conversation, relationship, and focus must be made clear and agreed upon. This holds true for every session, not just once at the beginning.

**Listening:**

This is what the coach does to actively understand needs.

**In the Adaptive Conversation Process,** this is intrinsically important as the coach will **call out the situation**. Active listening is an important skill to develop and lean on for effective conversations. In this step, the coach is listening to what the coachee is "seeing" versus "seeking" to firmly understand before moving the conversation forward. Whether single-goal or transformational in nature, verbalizing this distinction is critical in the coaching process.

**Exploring:**

These are the options and perspectives that the coach and coachee come up with along a transformative journey.

**In the Adaptive Conversation Process**, this is discovered through open dialogue as coach and coachee **consider possibilities** and **calibrate change**. Probing for options, challenging roadblocks, and exploring how to measure positive progression toward transformation all take place here.

**Review**:

This wraps and recognizes progress that has been made toward transformation.

**In the Adaptive Conversation Process**, this is validated when the coachee **commits to act**. Seeing transformation in coaching requires knowing what has transpired prior, which leads to what should ensue. Intentional prior actions are part and parcel to intended next steps, which are agreed upon here. Since transformation is a long-term endeavor, this step goes further by ensuring commitment is confirmed for both near-term actions and long-term changes.

## INTEGRATING THE ADAPTIVE CONVERSATION PROCESS WITH MENTORING MODELS

While mentoring is another very common type of relationship that engages in developmental conversation, we have found that interaction frameworks tend to be similar across the board. Often, most of the distinction can be found in the ways mentoring programs are crafted within individual organizations, and therefore the conversations themselves typically align with goals of specific programs. As such, rather than trying to find one-off models put in place by companies, or forcing differentiation just for the sake of it, we will focus on just two common "types" of mentoring models, or approaches.

By examining these two approaches, and understanding their differences, we can recognize the foundational tenets of each and how they are met when integrating them with the value and strength that the Adaptive Conversation Process offers.

## CONVENTIONAL 1:1 MENTORING

A conventional 1:1 relationship is far and away the most common approach to mentoring.

Organizations that establish mentoring programs, as well as those who engage organically on their own, typically set up a framework where a more established mentor guides an early-stage or less experienced mentee.

The mentor-mentee relationship and subsequent focus are set on a foundation of sharing, in which the (typically more senior) mentor shares specific experiences with the (typically more junior) mentee in a way that addresses targeted goals for mentee development. Conventional 1:1 mentoring includes:

## (1:1) One Mentor:

- How is the mentor more senior and/or experienced in that which the mentee seeks development?

- How is the mentor more senior or experienced in a way that matters for the development of the more junior or less experienced mentee?

- Why is the mentor the single best person to share experiences with this person?


## (1:1) One Mentee:

- What is the mentee specifically targeting as a goal for development, which will become the primary focus with the mentor?

- In what ways does the mentee seek to grow into and/or achieve development that the mentor has already developed or achieved?

- How will placement of the mentee with this specific mentor be both effective and efficient in achieving the target development or growth?


This approach to mentoring is grounded in a 1:1 relationship, with the more senior person (mentor) guiding the more junior person (mentee), along a specific path of growth.

The mentee is not always junior in age or in title, though this is often the case. The mentor may simply be more seasoned in a particular skillset or other area of accomplishment, in which the mentee is less experienced or less accomplished. This is obvious in cases of "reverse-mentoring."

Leaders who appreciate the conventional tenets of this approach could easily integrate them in dialogue using the Adaptive Conversation Process.

## One Mentor – One Mentee

In a conventional 1:1 mentoring conversation, the mentor spends ample time speaking or sharing, most often equally or more than the mentee. This is counter to what we find in coaching conversations, where the coachee does most of the talking.

**In the Adaptive Conversation Process**, the mentee might begin by expressing the goal or target for development, and in keeping with the structure and intent of the process the mentor should **clarify the purpose** both in terms of how the conversation will progress and why specific experiences will be shared.

As the conversation progresses, the mentor will typically ask questions to **call out the situation**, ensuring the mentoring session points in the right direction. Too often, mentors skip this step and begin sharing what they feel would be beneficial, without validating alignment with what the mentee is seeking compared to current circumstances.

As the conversation progresses to **consider possibilities**, the mentor and mentee explore what kinds of experiences most closely align with the goal for the session. The mentor shares these experiences in detail, both telling stories and asking questions to ensure ongoing alignment, probing for meaning making along the way.

Often, specific experiences in what the mentor did or how the mentor approached something in the past will generate interest in how the mentee might do the same going forward. This leads to **calibrating change** with respect to how the mentee will take new learning forward, and measure to what degree trying these shared experiences might lead to positive change and development of the target goal.

The conversation wraps with a **commitment to act**, in which both mentor and mentee confirm what happens next and how they will reconnect. This is important both for the mentee (who will try what was shared), and also for the mentor (as time and energy have been committed, so this commitment shows appreciation).

## GROUP MENTORING

A less conventional but popular mentoring approach is group mentoring. Organizations often find that they have a far greater number of individuals who seek development through mentoring relationships than they have more senior or experienced people to serve as mentors. This makes it difficult to provide effective mentoring to a broad population, often leading to mentoring only being made available to high-potential employees or to a smaller number of people overall.

Group mentoring connects a more senior or accomplished mentor with several mentees, at the same time, to address several growth objectives the group has in common. This approach meets the needs of a broader population, while also providing more opportunities for those who would like to mentor but may not have the time or desire to engage in a conventional 1:1 approach.

The key here is that multiple mentees receive mentoring simultaneously as a group, which is a flexible way to share experiences for the benefit and development of more people.

This approach is less personal than in conventional 1:1 mentoring, but it is much more scalable and therefore we see it as an element in many career development and leadership programs.

## Mentor:

What interest has a leader expressed in mentoring by sharing experiences, in a way that is valuable but limits the time commitment?

How is the mentor more senior and/or experienced in that which a group of mentees seeks common development?

How is the mentor more senior or experienced in a way that makes sense for the target development of the group of more junior or less experienced mentees?

Why is the mentor the single best person to share experiences with this group, collectively?

## Mentees:

How committed to the group mentoring setting are those who would participate, with expectation to engage and add value with the group just as they extract value from the mentor?

What target development does the group of mentees have in common, which makes sense for why they were grouped for mentorship in this way?

How do the group of mentees relate to the mentor? Do they commonly seek to achieve the same role as the mentor, promote to the same level of leadership, reach similar achievements or skill proficiency, etc.?

How is targeted development of each mentee in the group achieved effectively and efficiently in a scaled group mentoring setting as opposed to pairing 1:1?

## One Mentor – Many Mentees

In a group mentoring conversation, the best practices we have seen include a moderator that kicks off the session. The mentor often begins with an introduction that includes things such as title, role, tenure, and generalizations around the scope of how experiences will be shared to address why the group has been formed in a specific way.

**In the Adaptive Conversation Process**, it is in this introduction where the moderator and mentor will collectively **clarify the purpose** of the conversation they will have as a group. This sets expectations and allows everyone in the group to begin at the same point in the group conversation.

Since group mentoring addresses similar developmental targets shared by everyone present, the experiences shared will largely be focused within that scope; however, as the group is still composed of individuals, there will certainly be different reactions and requests to share for different reasons. Because of this, it is likely that more than one situation will be laid out, and more than one experience will be shared in a single group mentoring session. This is one of the few cases in which the linear approach to the Adaptive Conversation Process will flex. One or more mentees will **call out the situation** being experienced and the group will then engage with the mentor in **considering possibilities** for what kind of experience might be most appropriate to share. As the group listens, reacts, and discusses they will inevitably move on to another situation and possible experiences to be shared. This indicates that these two steps in the Adaptive Conversation Process may be viewed as one larger connected step, which may be toggled between for most of the group mentoring session.

As the group mentoring session nears the end of its set time together, often the moderator will step in to engage the group in the part of the conversation that **calibrates change**. This engages the mentees with each other as well as with the mentor and moderator, to forecast measuring how applying what they have heard might help them develop individually toward their own targeted development goals.

Often near the end of the session, when it is time to **commit to act**, the moderator may even facilitate an activity. Mentees might spend time individually contemplating what they will do next and perhaps share with the group. Another best practice we have seen is for mentees in the group to pair up as "buddies" or "accountability partners" to share how they are processing the experiences shared by the mentor and discuss how they plan to apply what they heard. Additionally, they may follow up with the mentor in a limited fashion to share how they have grown through their engagement.

Again, group mentoring is a much less personal or intimate approach and lacks the deeper relationship and connection between mentor and mentee; however, that does not make this approach any less effective. For many companies, outside of high-potential programs or succession development, group mentoring is the most effective way to achieve scale.

## INTEGRATING THE ADAPTIVE CONVERSATION PROCESS WITH TEACHING CONVERSATION MODELS

One of the most common questions we hear in leadership development conversations is around how to help people-leaders become better coaches. While this is very important, too often we find that the term "coaching" is used as a blanket for other types of conversations.

One of the most common misuses is when the true intent is for one person to help "teach" another person. There is a difference between teaching and coaching. As we have explored briefly, coaching conversations are more geared toward helping someone along a path of self-discovery. The coachee declares the goal, as well as alignment with it and the definition of success. They know the answer they are seeking, and the coach helps them self-discover it.

Conversely with a teaching conversation, the goal may be set by the person asking to learn or by the person doing the teaching. The outcome is less self-discovery and more direct explanation to achieve increased knowledge or ability. An expectation that has been set, whether small as in performing a task or large as in realizing a specific level of achievement, equals pre-defined success.

In teaching conversations, the person leading the conversation is helping another to "be able to" know and/or do something, either for the first time or progressively better.

Just as we explored with coaching and performance conversations, there are various models of teaching conversations. Again, we respect their tenets while showing how they can be integrated by following the practical steps in the Adaptive Conversation Process.

Let's look at a few common teaching models you may have seen before:

## TELL-SHOW-DO

The Tell-Show-Do model, often associated with Charles R. Allen who adapted the Herbart method during World War I, is a straightforward approach to teaching something to another person. It is often an approach we see in new-hire training. Someone (often a leader or subject matter expert) is ready to help them show that they can "do" what they have learned. This model has three easy steps, which are:

**Tell**     What the person is going to learn, do, and achieve.

**Show**     What the person doing the teaching will model.

**Do**     What the person being taught subsequently will perform.

While the Tell-Show-Do model is basic, leaders who follow its tenets (often because they are so obvious and simple) can integrate them with the Adaptive Conversation Process.


**Tell**:

This is informing what the person will learn, be able to do, and achieve after having been taught.

**In the Adaptive Conversation Process** this is the starting point, whether it has been learned formally already or if it is the first time being introduced to a task. The person leading the conversation must begin by explaining how the process of teaching will take place and then diving deeper into what is to be done. In the Adaptive Conversation Process model, this is where we **clarify the purpose** of the teaching conversation, as well as the learning objective.

**Show**:

This is modeling the way something will be done by the person doing the teaching.

**In the Adaptive Conversation Process,** this is where we **call out the situation**. The "teacher" might recognize an opportunity to exhibit a behavior or complete a task, and make this opportunity known to the person being taught. It is a chance for intentional observation as an interim step to application. The teacher often directly asks questions such as, "what did you see me do?" and "what was I trying to achieve in doing that?" to help the other person make a connection that will set the stage to move from knowing to doing.

**Do:**

This is what the person being taught will perform. It is moving theory and modeling to the next level by applying learning.

**In the Adaptive Conversation Process** this is where the rubber meets the road in teaching. This is often either an initial attempt to do something in a new way, or for the first time altogether. It is at this stage, once learners have attempted to do something themselves, that we then **consider possibilities** in a proactive and reflective manner. While applying what has been learned and seen, the conversation leader may proactively pause to ask questions such as, "what should you do in this case?" or "what is the next step in this situation?" After the behavior has been demonstrated, reflectively the leader of the conversation may ask questions such as, "what did I do that you could have done?" or "what got in the way of you doing something that needed to be done?"

These types of questions can also be pointed out if the person cannot answer them, which is another distinction of teaching. In the Adaptive Conversation Process, the point at which we **calibrate change** can be interactive along a path of learning. Since the individual will have moved from seeing something accomplished, to actively doing that which is being taught, iterative measurement of success should be observed.

These points in the conversation still should be summarized prior to the point where we **commit to act**, as this is the stage in which teaching moves toward closure – either as success has been achieved or perhaps where more instruction is still needed. Either way, outcomes are acknowledged and agreement on next steps is laid out with a commitment to practice, circle back if needed, and display the level of proficiency expected.

## INQUIRY-BASED LEARNING

Largely credited to American philosopher and educator John Dewey, Inquiry-Based Learning is grounded in questioning and actively probing for deeper exploration. Conversations aimed at teaching through use of this model focus primarily on the learner as central rather than the teacher as such.

While there are various representations one might construct to explain this model, our understanding of it would infer primary elements as follows:

| | |
|---|---|
| **Curiosity** | What questions can be asked to discover, design, or redraw meaning, understanding, or ability? |
| **Consideration** | What research, resources, or reflection might lead to new information or insights? |

**Construction**     What connection, combination, or
                     new creation can be built through
                     this investigation process?

While the inquiry-based learning model is grounded in a
century old learning theory, it certainly applies today.
Leaders who follow the model's tenets as we have inferred
herein can easily integrate them in dialogue using the
Adaptive Conversation Process.

**Curiosity**:

This is the desire to seek out deeper meaning and learn new
information that will improve or increase knowledge and
ability

**In the Adaptive Conversation Process**, this is an innately
personal endeavor. Curiosity may be triggered externally;
however, from a learning perspective it comes from within
and then can be shared. This is where we **clarify the
purpose** of the conversation and what is meant to be taught
(and learned), calling out an expectation for curiosity as a
lever for active engagement.

Curiosity also creates a connection between **calling out the
situation** and **considering possibilities**, with the latter
being perhaps most important.

**Consideration**:

This is the cognitive process of taking new information
gained and wrestling with it in a thoughtful manner.

**In the Adaptive Conversation Process**, this is where the
teaching takes shape. It is the process of weighing all that

being curious has generated, and what that means in a more tangible sense. In the process, this is where we move through **considering possibilities** tied to learning and then including time for **calibrating change**.

New information or insights will have been formed and will be ready to be tested in practice. Prior to active testing, consideration of the reliability and validity of new learning takes place in the conversation, measuring success within the teaching setting and gauging anticipated future success as well.

**Construction**:

This is the formal creation of new knowledge and/or abilities that have been learned.

**In the Adaptive Conversation Process**, this wraps the dialogue and signals readiness to move learning from a controlled environment to a live one. In this Process, this is where we **commit to act**, as new learning can only truly be confirmed in action. Confirmation of what will be done, and an agreement to apply new learning, closes the conversation.

## COOPERATIVE LEARNING

Though not directly tied to one learning theorist, John Dewey is also largely credited with the idea of building cooperation into learning.

Cooperative learning permeates learning strategies and techniques at all levels. At its core, this approach to teaching breaks away from direct instruction methods and embraces a cooperative approach. Our understanding of it would infer primary elements as follows:

**Shared Tactic**    In opposition to individual teaching, how will all involved parties contribute in a joint effort to learning?

**Symbiosis**    What is the simultaneous inter-reliant relationship between teacher and learner?

**Co-Creation**    What learning outcomes are achieved and committed to through partnered development?

While the cooperative learning model is a very broad-based approach to learning, often referenced in the context of a training program or larger learning initiative, it has application even in a one-on-one conversation. Leaders who follow tenets of this approach, as we have inferred herein, can integrate them in dialogue using the Adaptive Conversation Process.

**Shared Tactic:**

This is where a leader would approach teaching and learning in partnership with a team member, which is foundational to this approach.

**In the Adaptive Conversation Process,** this is where we would ground discussion in cooperative learning. This approach is very different than a conversation where a leader (primarily talking) would teach a team member (primarily listening) how to do something. In the process, this is where we **clarify the purpose** of both "what" is to be taught and "how" it will be done collectively as an intentional approach.

**Symbiosis**:

This is the inter-connected nature of both individuals engaged in a cooperative relationship. It is representative of how a leader would engage intentionally and actively across all facets of the conversation with a team member.

**In the Adaptive Conversation Process,** this is the point in which teaching is approached as a two-way street, with thought and subsequent learning building off that which is generated together. At this step in the process, we **call out the situation**, working in tandem to identify the current reality and flesh out a future preferred reality, and work together to address the gap between the two. In this approach, no one person owns the conversation, how thoughts expand, or how it takes shape, as it is a true partnership. Still, conversation benefits from structured progression.

**Co-Creation**:

This is the process of jointly forming new learning plans and actions. It is characterized by a collective go-forward expectation of that which has been taught and learned.

**In the Adaptive Conversation Process,** this is where most of the collective energy is focused, and where the partnership in teaching and learning grows. At this stage in the conversation, we **consider possibilities**, **calibrate change**, and **commit to act**. As an alliance to teach and learn together, tenets of co-creation are the most evident across these steps, and this is where the more active elements of the conversation take place. Following the Adaptive Conversation Process provides much needed structure to get the most out of the cooperative learning approach.

## INTEGRATING THE ADAPTIVE CONVERSATION PROCESS WITH PERFORMANCE CONVERSATION MODELS

Just as we explored with coaching, mentoring, and teaching, there are various models and approaches to performance-related conversations that many people find value in. Like what we have shared so far, we will outline just a few of those we see frequently in use. Through discussion and understanding, we respect their tenets while showing the flexibility to integrate them in the practical steps of the Adaptive Conversation Process.

Let's look at a few common approaches to performance conversations you may have seen:

## STAR

The STAR model introduced, by Development Dimensions International (DDI), focuses on feedback as a critical part of performance dialogue. Central to this model is a focus on specific behavior, framing it, and making addressing performance clearer. This model contains five stages, which are:

**S**ituation      What specifically is going on?

**T**ask      What led to the performance?

**A**ction      What has happened and/or been done?

**R**esult      What effect have actions had?

The STAR model, as a feedback-based approach, is one that brings to bear specifics of performance in a way that shine a light on effects. Leaders who appreciate these tenets could integrate them as they follow the Adaptive

Conversation Process, moving the conversation from what "has happened" to what "should happen" as well.

### Situation:

This is what specifically is going on that has prompted the discussion in the first place. It is the starting point.

**In the Adaptive Conversation Process**, this is the beginning as well, where we can **clarify purpose** by confirming the reason for, and goal of, the performance conversation. Knowing, for certain, the purpose of a performance conversation up front is crucial to successfully moving it in the right direction.

### Task:

This is what led to the need for a performance discussion in the first place. It is the context for conversation.

**In the Adaptive Conversation Process**, this is where we **call out the situation** and what is important to shine a light on. Here, we may find that what is occurring does, or does not, align with what is expected. The context is the gap that exists on the continuum between seeing and seeking. It is in this stage of the performance conversation that the lens opens wider so feedback can be received constructively.

### Action:

This is what has happened. It is where content begins to expand, grounded in concrete behavior.

**In the Adaptive Conversation Process**, a fair amount of time and energy at this stage will be committed to addressing actions and then **considering possibilities**. Performance conversations, while not meant to be a lengthy or intense two-way debate, do rely still on two-way feedback. Behaviors or actions that are the focus of the conversation must be addressed clearly yet also explore what led to them and where we go from here. It is also an opportunity to determine what may be in the way (in the case where problematic performance exists) or what has been overcome (in the case where positive performance is being acknowledged). In either case, actions and the circumstances they are creating must be both recognized and explored for root cause, making this step of considering possibilities important for past understanding and future expectations.

**Result**:

These are the effects that actions have on performance and help further cement the initial purpose of the discussion.

**In the Adaptive Conversation Process**, this is where we take those possibilities agreed upon and recognize how much it helps to **calibrate change** associated with those actions for expected change in performance. Here, we also make sure to confirm a **commitment to act** and agree upon next steps. Performance conversations are not always negative or seeking change (for instance when we recognize positive performance); however, they do circle back to purpose by way of future performance, either altered or continued. This step in the Adaptive Conversation Process closes a necessary loop.

## SBI

The SBI model, introduced by the Center for Creative Leadership (CCL), may perhaps be one of the most common frameworks used in performance-related conversations. This model contains just three parts, which are:

**S**ituation      What happened?

**B**ehavior      What actions were observed?

**I**mpact      What effect have actions had?

This is another feedback-based approach to performance discussions. It is a short and straightforward way to express the current state of performance, with respect to something very specific. Leaders who follow SBI tenets could integrate them easily while using the Adaptive Conversation Process, growing the conversation from generally one-way concise sharing to a clear conversation that leaves appropriate room for constructive two-way dialogue.

**Situation**:

This is what happened and has led to the conversation. It is where a performance conversation begins using this approach.

**In the Adaptive Conversation Process**, this is where we **clarify purpose**. It expands the "what" has happened by making clear the "why" and goal of the performance conversation. Based on the type of performance being addressed (positive or negative), this clarification may also set an intentional tone.

**Behavior**:

This represents those observable actions that led to the performance conversation in the first place. This is a pivotal part of the conversation using this model.

**In the Adaptive Conversation Process**, this is critical. It is one thing to address performance from a perspective or viewpoint; however, this model is meant to address performance in an observable manner, which is based in fact. This is the part in the process where we **call out the situation**, and in keeping with the tenets of this model that means being clear and speaking from a place of fact. It is also where the Adaptive Conversation Process goes further, allowing for the conversation to start down a path of being openly constructive, by not only sharing what we are "seeing," but to express (also factually) what we are "seeking" in performance as it relates to the situation.

**Impact**:

This represents the effects actions have had on someone or something. It is what makes the conversation meaningful. Performance is not just about doing what is expected; rather, it is critically inclusive of why certain behavior is expected in a way that shows connected outcomes.

**In the Adaptive Conversation Process**, this is where we have an opportunity to expand the conversation in a way that opens the door for appropriate constructive two-way dialogue.

When we **consider possibilities**, we have an opportunity to explore options and roadblocks that may have pointed behavior in a particular direction, creating resultant impact.

When we **calibrate change**, we can discuss how performance will, or may, be measured to help achieve expectations and have the intended impact.

When we **commit to act**, we gain firm agreement on the next steps, while also using the gravity of impact to reinforce the expectation of ownership and accountability.

## AID

AID is another concise performance-based discussion model. Credited to Max Landsberg, who detailed it in his book *The Tao of Coaching,* AID is used to address specific behaviors and/or actions. This model also contains just three parts, which are:

**A**ction            What specific actions or behaviors exist?

**I**mpact            What is the effect of those actions or behaviors on performance?

**D**evelopment    What opportunities exist to improve performance?

This model is like others but is unique in that it intentionally creates space for discussion around learning. Leaders who appreciate the AIM model can integrate tenets of discussion and learning as they use the Adaptive Conversation Process.

## Action:

This identifies what specific actions have occurred or behaviors have been observed. This is critical to any performance conversation.

**In the Adaptive Conversation Process**, this is where we make sure to **clarify the purpose** for the conversation before jumping right into what we have observed. Priming the discussion by setting the stage first helps a person to be ready to hear what will be said next, as opposed to listening for clues on why the conversation is being had in the first place.

Next, in this step of the **Adaptive Conversation Process** we can move to **call out the situation**. This is where we can now focus on the specific behaviors or actions that are being addressed. If behavioral adjustment is the goal, then being clear in what we are seeing versus seeking is of utmost importance.

This part in the process also creates space for constructive performance dialogue around options (those taken and those perhaps that may be chosen in the future), as well as roadblocks (those that got in the way or which may proactively be avoided on the road to expected performance). In the Adaptive Conversation Process, this is the point where we **consider possibilities**. In keeping with the tenets of this model, we can begin to explore opportunities for development.

**Impact**:

This represents the effect of actions on performance. It is still very important in the performance conversation, yet as you can see it comes here much later in the conversational progression. Perhaps it is to focus more intently on the impact of development as an important element in performance improvement.

**In the Adaptive Conversation Process**, this is the point where we begin to **calibrate change**. Influenced by impact as a primary driver in this approach, we can assess in advance how actions will be measured and correlate to results. When we gauge change in this way, and look through a lens of development, results and outcomes may become clearer.

**Development**:

This represents opportunities to improve performance. As part and parcel to the entire conversation, this approach expects that development be agreed upon in the performance conversation.

**In the Adaptive Conversation Process**, this is where we **commit to act**. Agreement on next steps with respect to a "go-forward" cannot be fuzzy if performance is to be impacted. Agreement and clear next steps are essential to closing a constructive performance conversation, enabling change, and confirming development.

# 4.1

# Pre-Conversation Readiness

## (PCR Tool)

## How You Prepare Matters

According to Fractl (a researcher that uncovers the science behind data-driven content) a whopping 85% of people are likely to prepare for a conversation – more specifically for a difficult one. You might expect this to be the case; however, like with other statistics we often examine with relation to output or outcomes, it is imperative to consider what this preparation includes.

Often, we have found that leaders prepare primarily based on things like what they want to say, how they want to come across, why the conversation is necessary, etc. This represents preparing for content or message; however, what is often missing is enough preparation specifically with respect to the (perceived) readiness of the other person, and of themselves. This is where our PCR Tool (Pre-Conversation Readiness) can be helpful.

## The PCR Tool

Begin by writing both your name and the name of the person you intend to talk with on the left. Across the top include three columns for:

1) Cognitive Readiness
2) Emotional Readiness
3) Change Readiness

| PCR TOOL | Cognitive Readiness | Emotional Readiness | Change Readiness |
|---|---|---|---|
| Your Name | | | |
| Other Person's Name | | | |

In preparation for the conversation, consider the following and then answer YES or NO in the PCR Tool for both you and the person you will talk with.

Think about the readiness of the person you will have a specific conversation with, as well as your own. Consider the statements (below) under each of the three facets of readiness, which will help gauge the degree to which you believe each to be true. Once you have given ample thought, enter either YES or NO in the PCR Tool for each.

## Cognitive Readiness

1a.   I believe the person I will have this conversation with can think reasonably so we may engage constructively.

1b.   I am prepared to think reasonably so that I may lead a constructive conversation.

2a.   I believe the person I will have this conversation with can handle potential unpredictability within the conversation logically.

2b.   I am prepared to effectively manage potential unpredictability within the conversation logically.

## Emotional Readiness

1a.   I believe the person I will have this conversation with has control of their current emotional state and can handle feelings that the conversation presents or creates.

1b.    I am prepared, based on my current emotional state, and can manage feelings within me that the conversation may present or create.

2a.    I believe the person I will have this conversation with can process emotional triggers that may arise as the conversation progresses.

2b.    I am prepared to navigate my own emotional triggers that may arise as the conversation progresses.


## Change Readiness

1a.    I believe the person I will have this conversation with is open to exhibiting willingness and desire to consider something new or different that they will do and will be committed to internalizing it.

1b.    I am prepared to model and be equally open to considering something new or different that I will do, and I will be committed to internalizing it.

2a.    I believe the person I will have this conversation with has the ability and capacity to externalize something new or different responsibly in their actions.

2b.    I am prepared to equally externalize something new or different that may be expected of me, as appropriate, because of the conversation.


To feel the greatest amount of confidence going into the conversation, you should be able to say "YES" in every column for both you and the other person.

If there is any place where you have said "NO," take some time to consider why as well as what you may do (within your span of control or influence) to be better positioned to shift to "YES."

**For instance:**

**Cognitive Readiness**

If you do not believe **the other person** is cognitively ready for the conversation, ask yourself if there is anything within your control that you might consider doing beforehand. Is there an opportunity to begin framing the conversation in advance? Is there a particular day of the week or time of day when you have observed the other person performing cognitively at their best?

If **you** are not cognitively ready for the conversation, ask yourself what a reasonable person might think about it and how that aligns with what you are thinking. Consider ahead of time how the conversation might track from a logical perspective. Proactively consider rationale that may be raised in the conversation, which may or may not be something you would have predicted.

**Emotional Readiness**

If you do not believe **the other person** is emotionally ready for the conversation, ask yourself if there is anything you may need to keep in mind, prepare more for, or even influence in a certain way. Is this person often highly sensitive during this type of conversation? What has worked well in the past to manage feelings when this person responded emotionally during conversations? How might unmanaged emotions get in the way? Are there certain landmines you are aware of that you may want to avoid? Is there anything else going on in this person's life that may impact their current emotional state.

If **you** are not emotionally ready for the conversation, ask yourself what may be causing your current emotional state and how that could impact your effectiveness, whether it is directly related to the conversation or not. Consider what may be triggering a potential decrease in your own emotional self-control, and what you can do in advance to manage it. Do you need more time to prepare, or perhaps reach out to a coach or mentor yourself?

## Change Readiness

If you do not believe **the other person** is ready for change (to whatever degree the conversation at hand may call for it), ask yourself if there is anything you may need to address ahead of time or even as part of early dialogue in the conversation. Do you have prior experience with this person that leads you to believe they may not be open to new ideas, ways, or possibilities? Is there a particular environment in which your conversation might create more openness? Does the other person seem to have the time, energy, or skill to engage in something different?

If **you** are not ready for change, ask yourself what you are willing and able to do, which may result from the conversation. Are you willing to take ownership of certain action items, just as the other person may need to? Do you have any preconceived ideas around what you may be asked for? Do you have the capacity to do something more, or differently, if needed? Are there resources you may want to investigate ahead of time to be prepared with if asked during the conversation?

The **PRC Tool** is meant to help set you up for even greater success in your conversation. By taking time to assess **Pre-Conversation Readiness**, you are making a commitment to conversational effectiveness even before you engage with the other person.

# 4.2
# A Few Conversation Outlines

# Using the Adaptive Conversation Process for a
## COACHING CONVERSATION

## Step 1: CLARIFY PURPOSE

- What would you like to focus on in our coaching session?
- What I'm hearing is that you'd like to XYZ...is that correct?

## Step 2: CALL OUT THE SITUATION

- How are you doing this today? What would you be doing ideally?
- How would doing this differently impact that ideal state?

## Step 3: CONSIDER POSSIBILITIES

- What have you tried? How has that gone? What else might you try?
- What would help you do this? What's in the way that you can remove?

## Step 4: CALIBRATE CHANGE

- How could you tell if that is working? What would you need to see happening?
- What does success mean? What would the result look like?

## Step 5: COMMIT TO ACT

- What's next? What did you say you're going to do first?
- How would you like us to proceed from here? How will we follow up?

166

## Using the Adaptive Conversation Process for a
## DIFFICULT PERFORMANCE CONVERSATION

### Step 1: CLARIFY PURPOSE

- I'd like to have a conversation about X performance/ behavior today.
- Our goal is: put it on the table, talk about it, and correct it.

### Step 2: CALL OUT THE SITUATION

- The expectation is "A" but what is happening is "B" and it's causing "C." Do you see it?
- Based on X, there is a disconnect from expectation Y.

### Step 3: CONSIDER POSSIBILITIES

- What's in the way? How can we find a way to correct this? What needs to change?
- What can I do to support you in turning this around?

### Step 4: CALIBRATE CHANGE

- How will we know behavior/performance has improved? What can we expect to see?
- What will this behavior/performance look like once corrected?

### Step 5: COMMIT TO ACT

- Are you prepared to make this change? Can you commit to this?
- I'd like to see A by B. If not going as discussed, we'll follow up with X. Does that work?

## Using the Adaptive Conversation Process for a
## MENTORING CONVERSATION

### Step 1: CLARIFY PURPOSE

- What would you like me to share in our mentoring session today? What are you hoping to take away?
- What I'm hearing is you'd like to hear my experience with "X." Is that correct?

### Step 2: CALL OUT THE SITUATION

- How have you experienced this today? How does my shared experience impact what you are looking for?
- Does hearing my experience impact what you are seeking?

### Step 3: CONSIDER POSSIBILITIES

- Have you tried anything I've shared? How did that go for you? What else might you try from what I've shared?
- Could how I've done this in the past work for you? How is what you might try different? How is it similar?

### Step 4: CALIBRATE CHANGE

- If you try something I shared, how might you tell if that works for you? What would you need to see happening?
- In hearing what success meant for me, does that resonate with you? What might the result look like if you tried what I shared?

### Step 5: COMMIT TO ACT

- What's next based on what I shared? What will you do?
- How will we share going forward? How will we follow up?

## Using the Adaptive Conversation Process for a
## <u>CONSULTING CONVERSATION</u>

### Step 1: CLARIFY PURPOSE

- What are you hoping to achieve through this consulting engagement?
- What is the problem or opportunity we are addressing? I understand it to be "X," is that accurate?

### Step 2: CALL OUT THE SITUATION

- What is the current situation you are experiencing? What are you trying to get at or accomplish that is different?
- What data or evidence do you have that highlights the gap between where you are and where you want to be?

### Step 3: CONSIDER POSSIBILITIES

- What are the potential strategies we could explore to close this gap?
- How might these different options work? In what ways might they address the main concern.

### Step 4: CALIBRATE CHANGE

- How will we track progress on potential solutions?
- What leads us to believe this will solve the issue? What indicators will we look for to confirm the desired effect?

### Step 5: COMMIT TO ACT

- What are the specific actions each of us will take based on this conversation?
- What clear next steps need to be outlined & agreed upon on how we will work and in what ways we will follow up.

## Using the Adaptive Conversation Process for a
## TEACHING/TRAINING CONVERSATION

### Step 1: CLARIFY PURPOSE

- What is the specific skill or knowledge you want to learn from this session?
- From what I hear, you want to firmly know "X" and be able to "Y," Is that right?

### Step 2: CALL OUT THE SITUATION

- Where are you starting from in terms of knowledge or skill level? What level do you want to achieve?
- What challenges have you had with this so far? How are you today?

### Step 3: CONSIDER POSSIBILITIES

- What techniques or strategies could we explore to help you improve?
- Considering your preferred learning style, would trying "X" help you learn better than "Y" would?

### Step 4: CALIBRATE CHANGE

- How will you measure improvement in this knowledge or skill?
- How will you know if your learning has translated into the knowledge or skill desired? What will success look like for you?

### Step 5: COMMIT TO ACT

- How important is learning this to you?
- What will you practice or implement? What actionable steps will we follow up on, and when?

**Using the Adaptive Conversation Process for an**
**ADVISING CONVERSATION**

### Step 1: CLARIFY PURPOSE

- What is the advice you are seeking?
- What specific decision or challenge are we discussing? I understand it to be "X," is that accurate?

### Step 2: CALL OUT THE SITUATION

- What is your current situation? What factors are influencing the decision you are making?
- What do you want to have happen? What relevant information might help or point in the right direction?

### Step 3: CONSIDER POSSIBILITIES

- What are your options at this point. What factors might we consider in making the best choice?
- To what degree do you want my advice on the best possible option? In what ways might my advice address your decision point?

### Step 4: CALIBRATE CHANGE

- What would success look like in this decision? How might success be gauged among options?
- How will you reflect upon & evaluate the path ahead?

### Step 5: COMMIT TO ACT

- How important is moving this advice to action? What is your next step based on this conversation, and when?
- Does this advice lead to an end-state, or do we need to follow up?

**Using the Adaptive Conversation Process for a
CHANGE CONVERSATION**

### Step 1: CLARIFY PURPOSE

- Do you know the change we will discuss, and its main components, so we can begin at the right place?
- Are you fully aware of the change, its benefits, risks of not changing, expectations around it, and why is it necessary?

### Step 2: CALL OUT THE SITUATION

- The current state is "A" but is changing to "B" with expectations of "C." Can you see the difference? Can you discern the new normal?
- What ways will adjust? What are the differences?

### Step 3: CONSIDER POSSIBILITIES

- What options do you have for implementing this change? How might you go about the change with respect to your sphere of control?
- What knowledge and ability do you need to make the change? How can we transition as smoothly as possible?

### Step 4: CALIBRATE CHANGE

- What can we expect to see because of the change? How will we measure success as the change is implemented?
- What feedback will show that the transition is effective?

### Step 5: COMMIT TO ACT

- Are you prepared to change? What will you commit to?
- When will we see the change in practice? How will we follow up?

# 4.3

# Deeper Applications

## APPLYING THE ADAPTIVE CONVERSATION PROCESS TO COACHING

Coaching is an integral part of leadership that focuses on helping someone explore ways to improve and grow. At its core, coaching is about individual change, and it is goal-focused, often on immediate skill development needs or addressing specific challenges. Leaders who adopt effective coaching techniques help individuals unlock their potential by guiding them through reflective and solution-oriented conversations.

The Adaptive Conversation Process is particularly useful in coaching because it provides a structured, repeatable framework for guiding conversations that lead to change, growth, action, and improved performance. It serves as a roadmap for the conversation and helps leaders facilitate focused and impactful coaching conversations that avoid drifting off course and help drive real results.

### Step One: Clarify Purpose in Coaching Conversations

It is critical in coaching conversations to confirm the purpose of the conversation up front because it ensures that both the coach and the individual being coached (the coachee) are aligned from the start. This is more than acknowledging that the purpose is "for coaching." Confirming the purpose means ensuring, as the coach, what the coachee wants to focus on and get at in that specific conversation. In coaching, the purpose is often focused on what the coachee is trying to solve, improve, change, or otherwise achieve. By clearly defining the goal of the conversation, the coach and coachee can focus attention on what is to be accomplished, through open dialogue.

Clarifying purpose also involves confirming expectations for the conversation. It is often a good idea to do this in advance of the coaching session itself; however, it can be done as part clarifying purpose. Since coaching is different than teaching or advising, for instance, it is imperative that the coachee understands how the engagement will feel, and what it will yield. A coach is not there to give answers or advise which direction to take; rather, a coach is there to ask questions and help the coachee consider perspectives on the road to deciding what to do, or try, next on their path to achieving their goal. When both parties are clear on the purpose, the conversation can proceed with greater focus and efficiency.

### Example Situation:

Olivia, the Director of Information Technology, was asked by one of her project managers, Joseph, for some coaching. He was having an easy enough time managing most of his projects; however, for the few with very large teams made up of fully virtual members, he was experiencing some challenges.

To begin the coaching session, Olivia asked, "What do you want to focus on today?" Joseph responded that he wanted to improve his ability to get larger virtual project teams to engage with each other more actively outside of their regular meetings. He shared that the work was getting done; however, team members mostly interacted only when he brought everyone together for Zoom updates and handled the rest of their work in silos.

Olivia was aware of the challenges around managing virtual teams and had many ideas even beyond what Joesph was sharing; however, she also knew that the best practice in coaching was to focus on one thing at a time, and make sure it was that which her employee was asking to address.

Using the Adaptive Conversation Process as her guide, Olivia knew how important it was to clarify purpose before moving forward in the conversation. She made sure to do this by responding as follows:

*"Thank you for giving me an opportunity to provide coaching on this for you, Joseph. What I am hearing is that individuals on large virtual project teams only seem to interact with each other during your Zoom meetings, otherwise working independently, and you would like to figure out ways to better engage them with each other outside of these regular meetings. Is that correct?"*

Olivia found that mirroring what the other person was saying was a great way to clarify, and confirm, that she understood the exact purpose for the coaching session. Once Joseph acknowledged that she was correct, they were able to move to the next step in the Adaptive Conversation Process. Had she misunderstood, this would have been an opportunity to clarify before moving ahead. This clarity of purpose helped moved the conversation in an appropriate direction and set up the next step where they would call out the situation in greater detail.

**Tips for Clarifying Purpose in Coaching:**

• **Ask the coachee to define their goal:** Be sure to ask the coachee what they want to achieve. This helps ensure that the conversation is not too broad for a single coaching session, and that it addresses immediate needs.

• **Restate the purpose:** Once specifics around the request and goal have been shared, restate it clearly and concisely to ensure both coach and coachee are aligned on the focus of that specific coaching conversation.

• **Set conversation expectations:** Clarify how the conversation will proceed and progress, noting that you will focus on the specifically stated goal. If the coachee decides to move away from that initially stated goal, the best practice is to pause and ask if the initial purpose has changed before going any further. Assumptions are the enemy of effective and efficient coaching conversations.

### Step Two: Call Out the Situation in Coaching Conversations

With purpose clarified, calling out the situation in terms of what the coachee is seeing versus seeking is the next step in the Adaptive Conversation Process. This involves first asking the coachee to articulate the current state that is creating or contributing to the challenge or issue at hand. In coaching, this step is essential because it allows the coach to help the coachee reflect on their current reality, before comparing it to what they would prefer that reality to look and feel like.

Using probing questions to allow the coachee to share what is happening  before asking what they would like to see happen is a reasonable progression in the coaching conversation. Once these have both been fully articulated, the coachee will usually be closer to bringing into view what the gap truly is. Only once this gap becomes visible can the conversation move forward constructively. This step is not about finding solutions, but about helping the coachee bring the current picture into view so they are ready to ideate effectively.

NOTE: All too often, leaders want to lean on their own experience and jump straight to solution for their employees. This is where coaching can break down and turn into teaching or advising. Resist the urge and allow the conversation to move to the next step in the Adaptive Conversation Process.

## Example Situation:

Carter, the Nursing Director, was coaching Alan, a newer addition to his team. Alan was having difficulty managing his time and workflows during shifts. He had recently been assigned to the MICU (medical intensive care unit) after having spent the prior three years in the emergency room. The MICU handles less critically urgent conditions such as infections or other problems that necessitate intensive monitoring but do not require emergency care. As such, the pace of work was a big change for Alan, and he was experiencing some challenges managing the timing of new, less critically intensive, workflows.

During their coaching session, after clarifying purpose, Carter spent time asking Alan questions that would flesh out the reality of his current situation. They defined what his days looked like in the MICU compared to what he was used to in the emergency room, and how the difference affected how he was feeling. The differences were very clear, and by talking through them out loud Alan was able to begin seeing what he might need to approach differently, particularly the way he would now handle time between active monitoring and patient interaction.

By calling out the situation and identifying the core issue in plain terms based on what he was experiencing, Carter was able to ground the conversation (in reality) before moving into a phase that would open things up to possibilities, which

178

could address the goal of the coaching session. Before they moved into the next step in the Adaptive Conversation Process, Carter again summarized what he was hearing and asked if Alan felt ready to look at the situation from a higher-level perspective and begin to ideate around what he might try to make him feel better and acclimate more effectively in MICU workflows.

**Tips for Calling Out the Situation in Coaching:**

• **Ask for the full picture:** The coachee knows the current situation, but sometimes being too close for too long can make it difficult to see clearly. Taking time to allow the full picture to be painted is helpful for both the coach and the coachee.

• **Don't fill in the blanks:** As the coach, particularly as a "manager-coach," you may already have a good understanding of the situation. Resist filling in the blanks or moving too quickly. In this step of the Adaptive Conversation Process, it is important to allow the coachee to paint the picture as they see things, not how you understand them.

• **Call attention to the gap:** Once it is clear on what the coachee is "seeing" versus what they are "seeking," the gap between the two should be relatively in focus. Coachees often want to move on in the conversation at this point; however, it is important to confirm that the gap is clearly understood. Asking the coachee to state (or restate) the gap can be helpful, as it allows the conversation to flow more seamlessly into the next step.

## Step Three: Consider Possibilities in Coaching Conversations

In most coaching conversations, once you have shifted from "calling out" to "considering," the time spent on possibility-generation will take up the largest segment of your time, comparatively. This step in the Adaptive Conversation Process is all about helping the coachee think creatively about how they might address challenges, develop new skills, or change their approach to achieve better outcomes though doing something differently. Since thinking precedes doing, effective coaches will help their coachees to "think" in new and different ways, which opens their minds to options and alternative ways of "doing" something previously not considered, which might help achieve their goal.

The coach's role in this step is to facilitate brainstorming and exploration through asking open-ended questions and avoiding any sort of steering along the way. It is easy for coaches to get caught up in where they think the conversation around possibilities is headed; however, the most effective coaches will maintain a neutral position and allow coachees to go down whatever rabbit hole of possibilities they choose.

Rather than prescribing solutions, the coach should encourage the coachee to keep pushing ahead in considering different strategies, diverse approaches, and new behaviors that could lead toward achieving their goal. Although the coachee is the one coming up with possibilities, it still feels like a collaborative exploration, while placing ownership of ideas with the coachee to take control of their development.

**Example Situation:**

Ezra, the Director of Sales, was coaching Amelia, a fairly new sales representative. Amelia had been falling short on her iterative prospect meetings in recent months, so she asked Ezra for some help. Knowing that performance-related challenges were important to address, Ezra asked Amelia if she wanted training, advice, or coaching, and he explained the difference between them all. Once they agreed that coaching was the best approach, they scheduled an hour to meet.

Once they clarified the purpose of that specific coaching conversation, and spent time calling out the situation, they moved into the phase of the Adaptive Conversation Process where they would begin considering possibilities. To kick things off, Ezra asked Amelia a series of open-ended questions as follows:

*"What have you been doing so far to schedule prospecting calls? How has that worked for you? What other approaches have you considered? What has prevented you from trying them? How might trying these approaches help? What have you heard other sales reps doing? What might you get if you considered those tactics? What do you need?"*

As it turned out, this step in the Adaptive Conversation Process was eye opening for Amelia. She thought that she was more restricted in how she was allowed to prospect than she really was. She also did not want to be seen by the rest of the team as someone who did not know what she was doing, so she resisted the urge to collaborate with other reps. By considering possibilities in an open manner, Amelia came up with several ideas on her own, which Ezra encouraged her to try. Within a matter of weeks, she had doubled her prospects and enhanced her relationships across the team at the same time.

**Tips for Considering Possibilities in Coaching:**

• **Ask open-ended questions:** An open-ended question cannot be answered with a simple yes or no. By asking questions that get the coachee thinking and expounding out loud, new perspectives can come into view, and the ideation process feels easier.

• **Ask questions that shift perspectives:** When we look at something from the same perspective or through the same lens for too long, it can be difficult to consider options. Asking questions that urge the coachee to take a different approach in how they think about possibilities can often open the floodgates for previously unconsidered alternatives.

• **Give feedback without directing:** This process can be exhausting for the coachee, while exciting at the same time. Once enough time has gone by in this step, it is a good idea to give supportive feedback so the coachee feels encouraged by the work they have done. At the same time, resist the urge to tell them whether any of their possibilities will work or not, or if they should even be on the table. Unless there is a real reason why something simply must not be done, give the coachee space to fully vet and try new things.

**Step Four: Calibrate Change in Coaching Conversations**

Setting a clear way forward by taking possibilities that surfaced and deciding on which strategies to put in place, diverse approaches to try, or new behaviors to begin will certainly help move the coachee from current to desired state; however, there is a bit of two-way meta-cognition in the conversation that is important as well. Meta-cognition is thinking about how we think about something. In this case talking about it, in a way that builds a mutual awareness and understanding centered around, "how will we know, that what we believe we will know, is true."

Confused? Think of it this way:

**Cognition in the conversation:** Thinking and talking about certain actions the coachee can take and the assumed positive correlation to goal-aligned changes and outcomes that should result.

**Meta-Cognition in the conversation:** Thinking and talking about the thought processes behind deciding on those actions and then fleshing out what the coach and coachee should see that indicates the assumed positive correlation exists.

This is an important critical thinking step. In a coaching conversation, the possibilities generated are, until tested, only assumed to be worth a try. Meta-cognition is a strategy in calibrating change in advance. It provides deeper conversational clarity of what the coachee has decided, and how that decision might play out.

This step is important to ensure that the conversation leads to tangible results through well thought through changes. In coaching, calibrating change during the conversation means helping the coachee see measured results in advance of taking actions. This aligns with Dr. Stephen R. Covey's assertion that everything that happens has been created twice, with the physical creation following the mental. By taking time to calibrate change, the coach and coachee can talk through the construction of that mental creation, seeing measured results, iterative or otherwise, as part of the (first) mental creation. This sets the coachee up for greater success in measuring actions in the (second) physical creation that is to come.

## Example Situation:

Olivia, the Director of Information Technology, was coaching Carmen, one of her IT managers, on improving his delegation skills. He had been experiencing challenges on cross-functional project teams he was leading during three recent application development sprints.

At first, when there was a small issue a team member could not figure out, Carmen would just figure it out himself in the name of modeling good teamwork. As the projects progressed, some team members found themselves falling behind in executing dependent tasks, which affected the ability of other tasks to be completed on time. Carmen found himself handling many of the tasks himself for the sake of time. Eventually, the amount of effort Carmen was putting in, doing things his team members needed to be doing, was just too much.

Their coaching conversation progressed well, and by looking at things a bit differently Carmen came up with one action and one behavior he would change immediately. Excited to get started, Carmen asked to wrap their coaching session up so he could get going; however, Olivia knew the importance of calibrating change, as an important step in the Adaptive Conversation Process. She led Carmen through a brief exercise that went something like the following:

*"Before we confirm the next steps, I'd like for us to calibrate the changes you have suggested.*

*A behavior change you suggested is to resist the urge to do that which should otherwise be delegated, correct? What does this behavior change look like? How will you know that this is improving your delegation skills? What will you see as a result if this is working?*

*An action you suggested is to address this directly with your team at your next project meeting, together as opposed to individually. What does this meeting look like? What will your team members' reactions be? How will you know if this meeting will yield the changes you expect from them? What will you see happening?"*

It would have been easy enough for Olivia to follow Carmen's lead and simply end the meeting so he could get started on his plan. He already said what he was going to do, and their possibility generation yielded two great ideas, so why not just get started and circle back later to discuss how things went? That would have been an option; however, it would have allowed Carmen to jump directly to the (second) physical creation without regard to considering what it all might look like and how he would know if his actions were yielding the greatest results. By calibrating change, he was best prepared to put his plan into action, with eyes wide open on measuring the results he expected.

### Tips for Calibrating Change in Coaching:

• **Promote critical thinking:** It is one thing to encourage ideation and discuss measurement; however, it is another thing altogether to openly discuss the process behind that ideation and plan for measurement.

• **Two creations are better than one:** Jumping to act does not necessarily mean success will not follow; however, seeing first that (mental) action in terms of measurement indicators, can help adjust and guide the real (physical) action when put in place with greater accuracy and assuredness.

• **Check back before checking off:** Coach and coachee should determine when and how they will reconnect to examine the degree to which actions are yielding expected results. Adjustments might need to be made, and checking in allows for additional discussion and recalibration before assuming the coachee's goals have been fully achieved.

## Step Five: Commit To Act in Coaching Conversations

An effective coaching conversation wraps up when the coachee is ready for the next steps that will be taken and feels a conviction to own their execution.

In the Adaptive Conversation Process, the commitment to act is the final door the coach and coachee walk though together before embarking on whatever it is that will happen next. It is not a time when the coachee nods in agreement; rather, it is when the coachee verbalizes each action to be taken and expresses a commitment to take them enroute to achieve their stated goal. The coach's role is to help the coachee outline a clear action plan and ensure that they have the support and accountability needed to follow through on their commitments. In coaching, this step is crucial for both translating insights and ideas into tangible results, and grounding next steps as something only the coachee can own.

A successful coaching conversation concludes with agreement, both on accountabilities and on mechanisms for follow-up meetings or regular progress check-ins. The coach should also offer ongoing support and encouragement to help the coachee stay motivated and focused on their development.

**Example Situation:**

Ezra, Director of Sales, concluded a coaching conversation with his top sales representative, Rose, by ensuring a firm commitment to specific actions.

Rose had always exceeded her goals, which felt great to her but left her wondering what more she could learn or accomplish. Having gone to Ezra to receive mentoring in the past, she thought it wise to ask specifically for coaching around how she might expand her skillset even in the face of exceeding sales results.

After a full coaching conversation, before letting Rose run out to her next prospect meeting, Ezra asked her to pause and commit to act. Rose looked a bit puzzled. Did Ezra not think she was serious? Did he not trust she would try the things they discussed? Then, as Ezra allowed the moment of surprise to pass, Rose realized what he was doing. Ezra wanted her to say what she was going to do out loud. Salespeople are often very observant, and this was surely a coaching technique Ezra was employing.

By verbalizing the next steps, Rose was making a commitment to herself in the name of development, and a commitment to Ezra in the name of appreciation for his time coaching. Ezra spoke out loud as well, committing to checking in with Rose after about a month, and to exploring her development further across additional coaching sessions. By establishing their commitments in this final step of the Adaptive Conversation Process, they both had a greater sense of comfort and anticipation for what would come next.

**Tips for Committing to Act in Coaching:**

• **Create an action plan:** Help capture what the coachee outlines for specific actions they will take following the conversation. Ask for confirmation of clear timelines and expectations to include.

• **Show dual accountability:** As follow-up meetings or check-ins are scheduled, commit to them and don't cancel unless completely necessary. As a coach, you are asking your coachee to commit and be accountable, so modeling this is important.

• **Offer ongoing support:** Let the coachee know that you are available for guidance and support as they act on their goals. Reaffirming your commitment to their success closes your conversation and makes it easy to pick up on the next.


**CONCLUSION:**

**USING THE ADAPTIVE CONVERSATION PROCESS IN COACHING**

Coaching is a powerful tool for unlocking an individual's potential and helping them achieve their personal and professional goals.

The Adaptive Conversation Process can be used effectively as a structured conversational progression for effective coaching sessions. This increases capacity for the coach to be fully present with their coachees, spend less time worrying about where the discussion should go and devoting more effort to be present in the conversation.

By clarifying purpose to focus attention acutely on what is to be accomplished though coaching, calling out the situation to bring a comparative picture into view, considering possibilities by opening the mind to options and alternatives previously not considered, calibrating change through deeper conversational clarity of what has been decided and how that decision might play out, and committing to act in ways that add conviction to execution, you can engage in truly inspirational coaching conversations.

## APPLYING THE ADAPTIVE CONVERSATION PROCESS TO DIFFICULT PERFORMANCE CONVERSATIONS

Providing tough feedback can be one of the most challenging aspects of leadership. Conversations where an individual's performance falls short of expectations require sensitivity, clarity, and structure. Leaders must balance honesty with empathy, addressing underperformance while maintaining the employee's dignity and motivation. Mishandling these conversations can lead to defensiveness, disengagement, or even a breakdown in trust.

The Adaptive Conversation Process offers a structured framework that can help leaders navigate difficult performance discussions in a way that is constructive, action-oriented, and respectful. It can help leaders create dialogue that not only addresses the immediate performance issue but also sets the stage for improvement and growth while ensuring the conversation remains on-track.

### Step One: Clarify Purpose in Difficult Performance Conversations

Once an appropriate environment and atmosphere has been established that will foster a constructive performance-related discussion, it is especially important to clearly and concisely clarify the purpose of the conversation. In times when this type of conversation is necessary, employees will usually know what is coming, or at least they will have some idea if communication has been transparent. This means that the employee may already be feeling anxious and may be crafting a version of what the conversation may look and feel like before any words have even been spoken. This is why concise clarity is so important. Lengthy explanations up front can create confusion in the mind of a nervous employee, and without a clear understanding of the conversation's purpose the employee may feel attacked or uncertain about what is about to happen. Clarifying the purpose of the specific conversation at hand helps both the leader and employee understand why the conversation is happening and what they can expect from it.

### *Example Situation:*

Olivia, the Director of Information Technology, was meeting with a team member, James, whose recent software implementation project had fallen short of expectations. James had been leading the project for the last six months, since the beginning of the year, and had trouble along the way with meeting deadlines, motivating the team, and delivering results that met the expectations of the project sponsor. Olivia had several conversations with James along the way, offering everything from coaching, to training, and even advice. For their conversation this time, she knew there needed to be a more formal and serious tone, as it was performance-based and would likely impact James' end of year review when the time came.

Olivia opened the conversation by saying:

*"James, I would like to take the next thirty minutes to have a conversation about your recent software implementation project. The purpose is to focus on your performance on this project, acknowledge what has not been executed as expected, and discuss any issues going forward. Since this project is one of your goals for the year and will be part of your year-end overview, I'd like to approach this conversation with an eye toward helping your performance get back on track for your next project."*

By clarifying the purpose of the conversation in no uncertain terms, Olivia set the tone for a serious, yet constructive, conversation that would focus on performance and possibilities to improve rather than excuses or blame.

**Tips for Clarifying Purpose in Difficult Performance Conversations:**

• **Be up front about the reason:** Clearly state why the conversation is taking place and what you hope to achieve by the end of it. Your employee might not like the reason for the conversation, but in the end will respect honesty and transparency.

• **Keep the focus on improvement:** Emphasize that the reality is that performance has fallen short; however, double-down on your purpose that you want to find ways to improve the deficiency. This brings something positive and supportive into a tough conversation.

• **Set a calm, professional tone:** Establish a serious, yet respectful and calm environment where the employee feels supported, even in a tough performance conversation. Adults do not want to feel as though they are being talked down to or punished, and leaders should not want them to feel that way.

**Step Two: Call Out the Situation in Difficult Performance Conversations**

Once the purpose for the conversation has been made clear, invest ample time to identify the specific performance issues that need to be addressed. Do this in a manner that explores facts, not feelings, about what was expected and what happened. It is important to be as specific as possible in this part of the conversation, using data, examples, or metrics to illustrate the performance gaps. By providing clear and objective information, leaders can help employees understand the deficiency more precisely without making the conversation feel overly personal or accusatory.

In difficult performance conversations, this step is crucial for avoiding ambiguity. Vague feedback can leave employees confused or unsure about what they need to change. Likewise, if the employee feels attacked personally, they will withdraw from any sort of constructive conversation and go in a very different direction. Instead, the leader should focus on factual inadequate outcomes and specific instances of underperformance, detailing how the employee's actions (or lack thereof) have affected the team, project, or organization.

### *Example Situation:*

Ezra, the Director of Sales, gave performance feedback to one of his sales representatives, Laura, whose recent sales figures had been significantly below target. She started the year with first-quarter sales that were in-line with benchmarks; however, her second quarter fell short of interim goals, and two months into the third quarter her sales numbers were still only half of what they should be. Ezra and Laura had prior conversations around change, as she was resisting new processes and technological features meant to increase leads and identify warm prospects. Her sales performance issue was due, in large part, to her reluctance to take advantage of new collaboration features in their client resource management platform.

Instead of making general statements about her performance, Ezra called out the specific situation:

*"Laura, we have had constructive conversations around change and how important it is for you to use our new CRM collaboration tool. Per CRM utilization data, in the last five months you have only used this tool in 15% of applicable prospective client outreach cases. Does that sound accurate today? As we have discussed, I expect you to use the tool 100% of the time in applicable situations. Do you see the difference here in what we are seeing compared to what I expect?"*

By providing clear, data that came straight from the CRM, Ezra provided Laura with facts she could not refute. Sometimes it just takes helping someone see clearly, in objective and absolute terms, before they can acknowledge the gap in performance.

**Tips for Calling Out the Situation in Difficult Performance Conversations:**

• **Use specific examples:** Provide concrete examples of the employee's performance issues, using data, metrics, or direct feedback. This helps to call out what you see in their performance at that point in time.

• **Avoid personal attacks:** Keep the focus on the employee's actions or behaviors, not their character or attributes. Concentrate on "what is" versus "what should be" from a purely performance, not personal, perspective.

• **Be clear and direct:** Do not dance around the issue. Your employe may already be nervous for a performance-focused conversation, so be clear in calling out the difference between what is happening and what you expect to be happening.

**Step Three: Consider Possibilities in Difficult Performance Conversations**

Once the performance issue has been identified in terms of the gap between what "is" and what "should be," the conversation can shift to the next step in the Adaptive Conversation Process, where the leader can engage the employee in considering possibilities to close the gap. It is easy for the leader to tell an employee what is expected; however, having a performance-based conversation assumes that expectation was already known, so exploring how the employee can close the gap is where the conversation must go next. This is where we often find the conversation hitting a fork in the road in which one path reveals inability, and the other path reveals unwillingness. This is where the leader and employee collaborate to find solutions, focusing on actionable steps that can lead to better outcomes and meeting expectations in the future.

In tough performance conversations, it is important to strike a balance between offering guidance and allowing the employee to take ownership of possibilities for improvement. Leaders should ask open-ended questions that encourage the employee to reflect on their performance and suggest potential solutions, except of course for certain extremely specific things the leader does want to see happen. This not only empowers the employee to take responsibility for their performance improvement but also fosters a sense of collaboration and empowerment.

*Example Situation:*

Molly, the VP of Lending, was addressing underperformance from one of her loan officers, Jacob, whose processing times were consistently slower than the team average. Molly and Jacob already had coaching conversations in the past, and Jacob paired with a tenured teammate to learn techniques and best practices, which improved performance for a few months. When Jacob's processing times once again trended down over the course of five weeks and started affecting successful workload management across the team, Molly knew it was time for a difficult performance conversation.

After setting a clear purpose for the conversation and calling out the situation, Molly shifted the focus of their dialogue to consider possibilities for improvement:

*"Jacob, what helped you improve processing time after spending time with a teammate? How did that work for you before? How has that approach changed? What have you tried lately? What are other ways you might improve your processing times? What tools or resources would help you speed up your workflow? What is getting in the way? How can I help yet you retain accountability?"*

By asking for Jacob's input as opposed to just telling him what to do differently, Molly engaged him in the process of creating his own success. She encouraged him to take ownership of the improvement process, while also offering her support in finding solutions, and being clear that regardless of which possibilities he chose to act on he would be accountable.

**Tips for Considering Possibilities in Difficult Performance Conversations:**

• **Encourage reflection:** Ask the employee for their perspective on what may be causing or contributing to their struggle. Resist the urge to jump at telling them what to try and instead give them space to reflect on what they think might help them improve.

• **Collaborate on solutions:** Work together to brainstorm potential strategies for improvement. Whether additional training, different resources, or changes in workflow if appropriate, by co-creating a list of possibilities there is an innate sense of buy-in from the employee to try something new.

• **Focus on growth:** Frame the conversation as an opportunity to gain experience and develop, rather than as a punitive measure. The purpose of the conversation is already clear that it is addressing a performance deficiency; therefore, over-focusing on negatives will only degrade the employee's motivation. By displaying positivity, leaders help generate motivation to improve.

## Step Four: Calibrate Change in Difficult Performance Conversations

The fourth step in the Adaptive Conversation Process, Calibrate Change, involves setting specific measurements that the employee can use to gauge the level of improvement in performance. In tough performance discussions, it is important that measurement of goals is realistic, achievable, and aligned with the employee's role and responsibilities. By calibrating change, the leader helps the employee understand what success looks like, what to look for iteratively, and how they can measure their progress overall.

In this step of the Adaptive Conversation Process, the leader should work with the employee to break down their performance improvement goals into manageable steps, setting clear timelines and expectations around what measurement should show. It is also important to discuss any support or resources the employee may need if they are to achieve expected measures of performance, such as additional training or mentorship.

### *Example Situation:*

Carter, the Nursing Director, was meeting with one of his floating nurses, Lily, who had been struggling with communication during shift changes. Being a floater, she often assumed that she could go where she felt the greatest need was; however, Carter had clear expectations of all nurses that schedules be confirmed and followed across the board.

After discussing the issue with Lily in a formal performance conversation and exploring possible roadblocks and solutions, Carter and Lily came to an agreement on how she would confirm, check-in, and check-out for floating shifts. Carter further helped Lily calibrate change by setting specific indicators she could look for that would tell her if she was meeting these expectations.

Over the next month, Lily focused on improving how she handled shift changes, making sure to validate success as she and Carter identified. Carter checked in with her weekly to review how she was feeling, and if the actions and measures were still working as planned. By setting clear, measurable actions that Lily could take, she had a roadmap for improvement.

## Tips for Calibrating Change in Difficult Performance Conversations:

• **Set specific measures:** Work with the employee to define clear actions that can be measured and tracked over time.

• **Break down actions into smaller steps:** Help the employee break down multi-part actions into more manageable bit sized action-items. This makes calibration easier and helps identify any adjustments that may be necessary without waiting too long.

• **Establish timelines:** Set deadlines or time frames for checking in on iterative measurements, for purposes of calibration or confirmation. Achieving each action and subsequent performance goal requires solid communication in the form of established progress review.

## Step Five: Commit To Act in Difficult Performance Conversations

The final step, Commit to Act, is where the employee commits to taking the actions necessary to meet the performance improvement goals, and the leader commits to providing ongoing support. In this phase, the conversation moves from planning and measurement to execution. Both the leader and the employee must be clear about the specific actions that will be taken and how progress will be tracked.

In tough performance conversations, it is crucial for the leader to reinforce the employee's accountability while also offering support. This may involve scheduling follow-up meetings, providing additional resources, or offering other assistance to help the employee succeed. The leader should also express confidence in the employee's ability to improve, helping to build their motivation and commitment to the process.

### Example Situation:

Ezra concluded a tough performance conversation with Laura, a sales representative, by asking her to commit to specific actions. Laura agreed to generate a larger list of questions to use in sales meetings, as she often found herself floundering and unprepared. This was identified as an easy approach to address deficiencies that were contributing to her lack of performance.

Their performance discussion focused on improving her qualifying questions during sales meetings, and Ezra committed to providing additional coaching and role-playing exercises after he could confirm that she was meeting iterative measures. The work Laura would do was meant to help her build questioning skills through added preparedness.

To close their discussion formally in-line with the Adaptive Conversation Process, Ezra asked Laura to repeat what she would do and confirm her commitment. They scheduled a follow-up meeting one month out to review her progress and adjust strategy if needed. By formalizing actions and commitments, both Ezra and Laura left the conversation with a clear understanding of the next steps and felt good about progress toward improving performance.

### Tips for Committing to Act in Difficult Performance Conversations:

• **Create an action plan:** Outline the specific actions the employee will take to improve their performance. Clarify verbally, and in writing where it makes sense, and be sure to include the leader's role in providing support.

• **Schedule follow-up meetings:** Set up regular check-ins to review progress, ensure the employee is doing what was agreed upon, provide feedback, and make any necessary adjustments to the plan.

• **Offer encouragement:** Reinforce belief in the employee's ability to improve. A difficult performance conversation does not have to feel negative. It can be formal and serious, while expressing faith and a commitment to help the employee succeed.

## CONCLUSION:

## USING THE ADAPTIVE CONVERSATION PROCESS IN DIFFICULT PERFORMANCE CONVERSATIONS

Difficult performance conversations are a necessary part of leadership, but they do not have to be adversarial or demotivating.

As a guide for tough performance discussions, the Adaptive Conversation Process provides both structure and space for leaders to convey the gravity of the issue while organizing and facilitating the conversation in a way that is respectful, constructive, and focused on improvement.

By clarifying purpose in a concise manner on what the conversation will address, calling out the situation in a way that explores facts, not feelings, about what was expected and what has happened to bring a comparative picture into view, considering possibilities that explore how the employee can close the performance gap whether due to an issue with ability or willingness, calibrating change to gauge the level of improvement in performance both iteratively and overall, and committing to act so the conversation can (importantly) move from planning and measurement to execution, you can firmly yet positively engage in effective performance conversations.

## APPLYING THE ADAPTIVE CONVERSATION PROCESS TO CONVERSATIONS WITH REMOTE AND HYBRID TEAMS

The shift to remote and hybrid work environments has been one of the most significant changes in the modern workplace. While remote work offers flexibility and increased productivity for many, it also brings new leadership challenges, particularly in maintaining engagement, collaboration, and communication. Leaders today must adapt their styles to manage teams that are often geographically dispersed across cities, time zones, and even spread around the globe.

The Adaptive Conversation Process is an invaluable tool in this context, helping leaders navigate these complexities by providing a clear, structured framework for ensuring meaningful and effective conversations despite the virtual distance. Whether addressing issues of team collaboration, employee well-being, or performance, the process ensures that conversations remain focused, empathetic, and action oriented.

### Step One: Clarify Purpose with Remote and Hybrid Teams

Particularly in remote environments, where messages sometimes lack real-time connection and interactions can tend to feel more transactional, it is crucial to start every conversation by clearly stating the purpose. This establishes an initial connection to the reason for the conversation – in that moment – and prevents misunderstandings that often arise from a lack of non-verbal cues such as body language, which play a significant role in face-to-face interactions.

Without the benefit of informal office interactions, where intentions can be clarified in real-time, remote conversations can quickly veer off track if not initiated with a clear purpose up front. Leaders should make a habit of beginning every important conversation by explicitly stating the reason and goal right away and ensuring that reason is clearly understood. This is true for team meetings just as it is for one-on-one conversations.

**Example Situation:**

Ezra, the Director of Sales, was leading a sales team spread across several states, all working remotely. He held weekly virtual team meetings, meant to discuss upcoming sales tactics; however, he noticed that the conversations often spun into operational issues and rarely touched on their specific sales strategies. To address this, Ezra started every meeting by explicitly stating that the purpose was to align key sales tactics for the week ahead. Whenever the conversation would drift into other topics, Ezra always had that initially stated purpose to point back at, bringing the conversation back on track and saving other topics for other meetings or conversations. This small change led to more focused discussions, with fewer tangential conversations. It also established the purpose for subsequent conversations with individual sales team members.

**Tips for Clarifying Purpose with Remote and Hybrid Teams:**

• **Send meeting agendas ahead of time:** This gives participants an initial view into the purpose of conversations, and a clear understanding of what will be discussed, helping them come prepared and stay on track.

• **Start with a purpose statement:** At the beginning of the meeting, articulate the purpose in clear terms, such as *"We are here today to discuss upcoming sales tactics and how we can streamline our sales pipeline."*

• **Check for understanding:** Always ensure that your team is aligned by asking if the purpose is clear to everyone.

### Step Two: Call Out the Situation with Remote and Hybrid Teams

In hybrid teams, where some members work from the office while others work remotely, it is important to call out any potential gaps or misalignments in the work dynamic that might impact conversations. This means taking stock in how the current state may affect the expected future state with respect to your conversation's purpose among differently placed team members. It also identifies gaps and creates transparency, helping to prevent feelings of exclusion, especially among remote employees who might feel disconnected from in-office colleagues.

Leaders should explicitly acknowledge the differences between remote and in-office experiences, making space for open discussions about challenges and frustrations. This not only validates the experiences of remote workers but also fosters a culture of inclusivity.

### Example Situation:

Carter, the Nursing Director, noticed that his hybrid team was experiencing communication breakdowns between on-site nurses and those providing telehealth services from home. He pulled the full team together to address the issue.

In this team meeting, after establishing a clear purpose, he called out the current situation directly:

*"I understand that those of you on-site have expressed a bit of frustration, and those of you working remotely have shared that you sometimes feel left out of the in-person decision-making happening on the floor. Let's discuss how we communicate today, how we want to communicate effectively with each other going forward, and how we might keep everyone in the loop regardless of location."*

By openly addressing the issue, Carter established a baseline and created space for an effective conversation, where team members felt comfortable sharing their concerns. This led to improved communication practices.

**Tips for Calling Out the Situation with Remote and Hybrid Teams:**

• **Acknowledge the disparity:** Don't shy away from addressing current state vs optimal state, or from calling out the different experiences of remote and in-office workers.

• **Create equal opportunities for input:** Ensure that remote workers have opportunities to contribute just as those in the office do, whether in brief conversations, regular meetings, or through everyday communications.

• **Encourage transparency:** Make sure your team feels safe to discuss the challenges they face in a remote or hybrid setting. Psychological safety leads to openness. Openness leads to communication. Communication leads to fuller conversations, which yield a treasure trove of trust and opportunity.

## Step Three: Consider Possibilities with Remote and Hybrid Teams

One of the biggest challenges for remote and hybrid teams is maintaining a sense of connection and camaraderie. Virtual environments can breed feelings of isolation, and without intentional efforts employees may feel disconnected from their colleagues and the organization. The third step in the Adaptive Conversation Process, Consider Possibilities, is particularly powerful in this context. It encourages leaders to explore creative ways to foster connection and collaboration in virtual spaces, giving a voice to everyone no matter where they may be situated.

Leaders should actively engage their teams in brainstorming ideas to strengthen their bond and improve communication, while maintaining focus on a conversation's initially established purpose. This could include implementing regular virtual "water cooler" sessions, organizing team-building activities, or rotating responsibilities to give everyone a sense of ownership in maintaining team morale. The Adaptive Conversation Process framework can even be displayed on a shared screen, so everyone knows which step the conversation is in, helping keep ideas flowing and the discussion on track.

### Example Situation:

Molly, the VP of Lending, noticed that her team, now fully remote, was losing its sense of community. She scheduled a virtual "team lunch" every two weeks where everyone could bring their meals and chat informally. Over time, this became a highlight for the team. One day, during one of these lunches, a team member suggested adding a trivia game to the sessions, which not only boosted engagement but also helped the team bond over friendly competition. As the purpose for these meetings was established up front, an openness to considering new possible ways for virtual engagement became the norm. Molly even found that some team members who had previously been silent became more vocal in ways that offered new perspectives, connected the leader with the team, and engaged everyone.

## Tips for Considering Possibilities with Remote and Hybrid Teams:

• **Schedule informal check-ins:** These can be as simple as virtual coffee breaks or lunches, where team members can chat about non-work topics. Remember, purpose is key to keeping the exploration of possibilities on track.

• **Encourage team-led activities:** Give team members the opportunity to lead discussions or activities, fostering a sense of belonging. Even consider sharing the Adaptive Conversation Process with the person leading the discussion.

• **Leverage collaboration tools:** Use tools like Slack or Microsoft Teams to create informal channels for sharing fun content, such as memes or photos, to maintain a sense of camaraderie. Your team and organization's culture and norms can help guide what is appropriate for you.

## Step Four: Calibrate Change with Remote and Hybrid Teams

In a remote environment, it is easy for leaders to lose touch with the day-to-day challenges their team members face. This is where regular feedback sessions come in. Without consistent feedback, small issues can snowball into larger problems, and remote employees can feel unsupported or left out of key decisions. The Adaptive Conversation Process emphasizes the importance of Calibrating Change, which in a remote setting translates to maintaining structured feedback sessions, and openly gauging measures regularly.

Leaders should set up frequent one-on-ones or team meetings to check in on progress, identify roadblocks, and offer support. This feedback should be both directional (providing guidance) and inquiry-based (asking team members about their experiences and challenges).

**Example Situation:**

Olivia, the Director of Information Technology, realized that her remote engineers were struggling with unclear expectations around deadlines and project milestones. To address this, she set up bi-weekly one-on-one check-ins to calibrate progress and clarify goals. She intentionally included opportunities for two-way feedback, which focused both on possibilities and gauging the reliability and validity of actions being measured. In doing so, Olivia found that her remote engineers both validated measures and recognized where disconnects may be occurring before they seriously impacted deadlines. These sessions allowed her to recalibrate and adjust measures as needed and ensure that her team members felt supported in their roles.

**Tips for Calibrating Change with Remote and Hybrid Teams:**

• **Schedule regular check-ins:** These can be weekly or bi-weekly, depending on projects and the team's needs, but they should be consistent. Even the timing and flow of these conversations themselves should be calibrated from time to time to ensure optimal effectiveness.

• **Use both directional and inquiry-based feedback:** Offer guidance where needed but also ask open-ended questions to uncover potential challenges. Conversations flow best when there is room for everyone's voice.

• **Create a feedback culture:** Encourage your team to provide feedback to you as well, fostering a two-way communication channel. Again, this helps to calibrate current and future conversations, meetings, and expectations.

## Step Five: Commit To Act with Remote and Hybrid Teams

In remote and hybrid teams, collaboration tools are the lifeblood of communication and workflow management; however, simply having these tools is not enough. Leaders must ensure that they are used effectively. The final step in the Adaptive Conversation Process, Commit to Act, is critical in this context. Leaders must commit to choosing the right tools for the team's needs and ensuring that everyone is trained and comfortable using them.

This step also involves setting clear expectations for how these tools will be used. For example, will Slack be used for informal communication, while email is reserved for more formal updates? How often should project management tools like Asana or Trello be updated? By establishing these norms, leaders can prevent confusion and ensure smoother collaboration.

**Example Situation:**

After a series of missed deadlines and miscommunications, Molly, the VP of Lending, realized her team was struggling with managing remote workflows. She committed to implementing a project management tool and led training sessions to ensure everyone knew how to use it effectively. Importantly, Molly also worked collaboratively with her team to establish collectively agreed upon expectations around who would enter work, and when, establishing a sense of ownership and accountability. Within a month, the team saw significant improvements in communication and accountability, as everyone had a clear view of project timelines and responsibilities.

**Tips for Committing to Act with Remote and Hybrid Teams:**

• **Choose the right tools:** Identify the tools that best suit your team's communication and workflow needs. Before adding a new tool, consider bringing the team into the vetting and decision-making process.

• **Set clear usage guidelines:** Ensure everyone knows when and how to use each tool. Employ solid change management practices when implementing to help team members engage successfully.

• **Invest in training:** Make sure your team is proficient in using the chosen tools to maximize their potential. Training does not have to be extensive, depending on the tool; however, setting aside time for this is important as some team members may feel more confident in using tools than others, yet not everyone feels equally as comfortable raising questions or sharing their feelings.

**CONCLUSION:**

## LEADING REMOTE AND HYBRID TEAMS WITH THE ADAPTIVE CONVERSATION PROCESS

Leading remote and hybrid teams requires a thoughtful and adaptable approach to communication.

The Adaptive Conversation Process offers a structured framework that helps leaders navigate the unique challenges of virtual leadership and conversations with geographically dispersed teams.

By focusing on clarifying purpose across meetings, calling out the situation and gaps to address, considering possibilities for connection, calibrating change through feedback loops, and committing to act using effective methods and tools, leaders can foster a productive, engaged, and cohesive team - no matter where they are located.

## APPLYING THE ADAPTIVE CONVERSATION PROCESS TO CROSS-CULTURAL LEADERSHIP IN GLOBAL TEAMS

In an increasingly globalized world, leaders are more likely to manage teams composed of individuals from diverse cultural backgrounds. Whether working with international colleagues, managing a globally distributed team, or leading projects across different countries, leaders must adapt their conversational strategies to address cultural nuances effectively. This requires a heightened awareness of cultural norms, communication styles, and values that influence how team members interact, make decisions, and respond to leadership.

The Adaptive Conversation Process is a powerful tool in navigating these complexities. Applying its structured yet flexible approach can help leaders ensure that their conversations are inclusive, culturally sensitive, and conducive to team cohesion and productivity.

### Step One: Clarify Purpose with Cross-Cultural Global Teams

Clarifying the purpose of a conversation is essential in any leadership context, but it becomes even more critical in cross-cultural settings. Misunderstandings can easily arise due to differences in how cultures interpret authority, directness, and expectations. For instance, in some cultures, direct communication is valued, while in others, it may be seen as too confrontational. Leaders must be especially mindful of how they frame the purpose of a conversation, ensuring that their message is clear and that cultural differences are acknowledged.

When working with a global team, it is important to state the purpose of a meeting or conversation in a way that resonates with all participants, regardless of their cultural background. This may involve providing more context, asking open-ended questions to ensure understanding, or adapting the level of directness based on the cultural expectations of the group.

**Example Situation:**

Ezra, the Director of Sales, manages a global sales team with members in the U.S., Germany, and Japan. He noticed that during meetings, his American and German colleagues were quick to jump into discussions about targets and metrics, while his Japanese colleagues often remained quiet. Ezra realized that his more direct approach to conversations was not resonating with his Japanese team members, who preferred a more consensus-driven style. To address this, he began each meeting by explicitly stating the purpose in a way that was inclusive for all team members, allowing time for everyone to reflect and provide input.

**Tips for Clarifying Purpose with Cross-Cultural Global Teams:**

• **Adapt the level of directness:** Be mindful of cultural preferences in direct versus indirect communication. In some cultures, direct feedback when clarifying purpose is expected, while in others a more subtle approach is preferred.

• **Provide additional context:** In cultures where hierarchy or formality is important, providing more context around the purpose can help team members feel comfortable and more prepared to contribute to the conversation.

• **Ask for feedback:** To ensure that the purpose of the conversation is clear across cultural lines, ask open-ended questions to invite feedback and clarification from all participants.

### Step Two: Call Out the Situation with Cross-Cultural Global Teams

When leading cross-cultural teams, it is important to recognize and call out cultural differences in a way that promotes understanding and inclusion. Cultural differences can impact how individuals express themselves, how they engage in discussions, and how they interpret leadership. Acknowledging these differences openly, rather than ignoring or glossing over them, helps create a respectful and inclusive environment where all team members feel valued.

Leaders should address cultural dynamics head-on, respecting where people are, compared to where the conversation is meant to go, creating space for team members to share how they prefer to communicate and work. This can also involve setting ground rules for meetings that ensure equal participation and encourage the expression of diverse perspectives.

### Example Situation:

Carter, the Nursing Director, was tasked with leading a healthcare project that included nurses from the U.S. and India. During early meetings, he noticed that the American nurses were much more vocal, while the Indian nurses tended to defer to their American colleagues even though they had perspectives on what they were seeing versus what the conversation was seeking, very valuable insights to share. Carter decided to call out this cultural dynamic during a meeting, explaining that different communication styles were at play and that he wanted to ensure everyone felt comfortable speaking up. He also implemented a practice where team members took turns leading discussions, which created respectful space for Indian nurses to take a more active role.

### Tips for Calling Out the Situation with Cross-Cultural Global Teams:

• **Acknowledge cultural differences:** Don't shy away from discussing cultural differences openly. Acknowledging these dynamics shows that you are aware and respectful of different perspectives.

• **Encourage equal participation:** Create a space where all voices are heard by actively encouraging quieter team members to contribute.

• **Set inclusive ground rules:** Establish norms for meetings that promote fairness, such as giving each team member an opportunity to lead discussions or limiting the time each person speaks to ensure balanced participation.

### Step Three: Consider Possibilities with Cross-Cultural Global Teams

One of the key challenges in managing cross-cultural teams is fostering a sense of inclusivity. In global teams, different cultural norms can lead to misunderstandings, misinterpretations, or feelings of exclusion. Leaders must actively explore possibilities to create an environment where all team members feel included, respected, and empowered to contribute.

The Adaptive Conversation Process encourages leaders to consider possibilities for inclusivity by engaging in open dialogue with their team members. This may involve asking for input on how the team can work more effectively together, exploring different cultural approaches to problem-solving, or finding ways to celebrate the diversity within the team.

**Example Situation:**

Olivia, the Director of Information Technology, led a multinational team that included engineers from Europe, Asia, and Latin America. She noticed that in team meetings, her European and Latin American engineers were more comfortable sharing ideas, while her Asian engineers tended to remain silent. Olivia engaged the team in considering possibilities for fostering a more inclusive environment by asking each team member how they preferred to communicate and contribute. She learned that her Asian engineers felt more comfortable sharing ideas in written form rather than during live meetings.

To accommodate this, she implemented a practice where team members could submit written suggestions before meetings, which were then discussed as part of the agenda. This tactic led to an increase in the number of options and possibilities to consider, generating a number of new ideas that were implemented with great success.

**Tips for Considering Possibilities with Cross-Cultural Global Teams:**

• **Explore different communication preferences**: Ask team members how they prefer to communicate, brainstorm, and contribute. Then, adapt your approach accordingly to include everyone's voice in the manner that best draws it out.

• **Rotate leadership roles:** Encourage inclusivity by rotating leadership roles in meetings, giving each team member the opportunity to lead conversations and share perspectives.

• **Celebrate diversity:** Recognize and celebrate the diversity within your team by acknowledging cultural holidays, customs, and traditions. This helps build a sense of belonging and respect among team members. That respect and connectedness can carry forward into future conversations, as well as build trust to contribute thoughts whenever considering possibilities.

**Step Four: Calibrate Change with Cross-Cultural Global Teams**

Calibrating change in a cross-cultural setting involves being sensitive to how different cultures approach and perceive constructive conflict, feedback, performance, and improvement. Some cultures embrace constructive conflict regardless of rank or position, whereas some have very different views on when or to what degree such conflict would be appropriate from a less senior or lower position. In some cultures, direct feedback is expected and welcomed, while in others, it can be seen as harsh or inappropriate. Leaders must navigate these cultural differences carefully, ensuring that feedback is delivered in a way that is both effective and culturally appropriate.

The Adaptive Conversation Process emphasizes the importance of adjusting feedback, performance, and measurement expectations to fit and consider the cultural context. Leaders should take time to understand how different team members interpret and act on feedback and be prepared to adapt their approach to ensure that desired outcomes are achieved.

**Example Situation:**

Ezra, the Director of Sales, was working with a global sales team that included members from Germany and China. He noticed that his German sales team was very results-oriented and expected direct feedback on their performance and metric achievement, while his Chinese team was more focused on maintaining harmony and preferred feedback to be delivered in a more indirect way.

To calibrate change effectively, Ezra tailored his feedback style based on these cultural preferences. For his German team, he provided clear, direct feedback during performance conversations, while for his Chinese team, he used a more indirect approach, framing feedback as suggestions for improvement rather than criticism. These approaches also helped to draw out nuances in conversations around measuring for success. His German team was already quick to point out variables that might not fit for accurate measurement, but only after adjusting his conversational approach was Ezra able to effectively engage his Chinese team members in sharing how their view of certain measures differed and might call for calibration.

**Tips for Calibrating Change with Cross-Cultural Global Teams:**

• **Tailor feedback based on cultural preferences:** Be mindful of how different cultures interpret feedback and adapt your approach accordingly. It is perfectly acceptable to ask if you are unsure. It shows that you care about and respect cultural differences in how you engage in conversations.

• **Use culturally appropriate language:** In cultures where direct criticism is frowned upon, use softer language and frame feedback as suggestions for improvement. Authenticity is critical here, as cultural awareness as a genuine approach in conversations is of utmost importance.

• **Encourage reflection:** In cultures that value consensus and reflection, give team members time to process feedback before expecting immediate action or responses. Calibrate your approach and expectations just as you would expect your team's calibration of measured actions to achieving outcomes.

**Step Five: Commit To Act with Cross-Cultural Global Teams**

In cross-cultural teams, committing to action involves more than just setting goals or expectations. It requires a commitment to ongoing learning and cultural understanding. Where some cultures will readily move on to the next actions based on the leader's call for it, other cultures will expect a more partnered approach to agreement. Leaders must be proactive in developing their own cultural competence and ensuring that their team members are equipped to work effectively across cultural boundaries.

This commitment may involve investing in cross-cultural training for both leaders and team members, establishing regular opportunities for cultural exchange, or creating a team charter that outlines expectations for communication, collaboration, and respect across cultures.

### Example Situation:

Carter, the Nursing Director, found that some nurses on his team were proficient across the board at gaining commitment from their patients to taking appropriate next steps with respect to post-surgical care and in-home instructions. Others on his team seemed to struggle in these conversations across certain cultural demographics, resulting in confusion or frustration. Carter wanted to ensure that his team was well-equipped to navigate the cultural dynamics of working with patients from diverse backgrounds. He committed to providing cross-cultural training for his team, focusing on how cultural norms can influence patient communication, particularly when engaging in conversations where commitment to act was vital to patient care. He also established a team charter that outlined the expectations for how team members would interact with each other and with patients from different cultural backgrounds. This not only improved the team's ability to work effectively across cultures, but it also enhanced patient outcomes by fostering more culturally sensitive care, and increased patient satisfaction scores broadly.

### Tips for Committing to Act with Cross-Cultural Global Teams:

• **Invest in cross-cultural training:** Provide training for your team on how to navigate cultural differences in communication, collaboration, and decision-making. Cultural sensitivity in conversations can make a world of difference.

• **Establish a team charter:** Create a charter that outlines expectations for respectful and inclusive communication across cultures. This should include cultural consideration with external customers as well as with each other.

• **Encourage ongoing learning:** Foster a culture of continuous learning by encouraging team members to share their cultural experiences and insights with each other, as well as their experiences having conversations with various culturally diverse groups

## CONCLUSION:

## NAVIGATING CROSS-CULTURAL LEADERSHIP AND GLOBAL TEAMS WITH THE ADAPTIVE CONVERSATION PROCESS

Leading cross-cultural teams requires an understanding of how cultural differences influence conversations, decision-making, collaboration, engagement, and communication.

The Adaptive Conversation Process provides a structured yet flexible approach to navigating these challenges as you engage in meaningful discussions, ensuring that leaders can foster an inclusive, respectful, and productive environment.

By clarifying purpose through framing, calling out the situation with respect for cultural dynamics, considering possibilities through inclusivity, calibrating change in ways that are important across cultural differences, and committing to act with cross-cultural understanding around direct vs partnered expectations, leaders can engage more effectively in conversations with diverse teams and best achieve organizational goals.

## APPLYING THE ADAPTIVE CONVERSATION PROCESS TO NAVIGATING DIGITAL COMMUNICATION PLATFORMS

The rise of digital communication platforms such as Zoom, Slack, Microsoft Teams, and Asana has transformed how groups collaborate and communicate. While these tools offer unprecedented flexibility and connectivity, they also introduce new challenges for leaders. Managing a team through screens, chat apps, and email threads requires a shift in how leaders facilitate conversations, maintain engagement, and drive productivity.

In this digital-first environment, the Adaptive Conversation Process can be seamlessly integrated into virtual interactions, ensuring that conversations remain clear, purposeful, and action-oriented, despite the absence of in-person cues. Leaders must adapt their communication styles to maximize the effectiveness of these platforms, creating a sense of structure, clarity, and connection when conversations are entirely virtual or even asynchronous.

### Step One: Clarify Purpose in Digital Communication

In digital communication, where messages can easily be misinterpreted, especially in written formats like email or chat, clarifying the purpose of each interaction becomes paramount. Digital conversations often lack the richness of face-to-face interactions, where body language, tone, and facial expressions can help convey meaning. Additionally, humans tend to apply their own meaning to digital communications they have received, often unconsciously, which may or may not align with the sender's true intent. As a result, leaders must be explicit about the purpose and goals of each conversation to ensure everyone is on the same page.

When using tools like Slack or Microsoft Teams, where conversations can become fragmented, it is important to start each discussion by clearly stating its objective. Whether having a team-wide Zoom call or sending a quick message in a group chat, clarity of purpose prevents confusion and ensures that every participant knows what to expect and how to contribute.

## Example Situation:

Olivia, the Director of Information Technology, was managing a global platform implementation project where much of the communication happened on Microsoft Teams. She noticed during important group conversations, that some team members would get sidetracked in chat threads, discussing tangential or even unrelated issues instead of focusing on the intended purpose of the conversation. To improve purpose clarity and curb this behavior, Olivia began every message or thread with a clear purpose statement, such as:

*"We are using this thread specifically to discuss the implementation timeline for Project Alpha. Please keep responses focused on this topic and use our digital parking lot for items we might address separately."*

This helped streamline conversations, keeping them organized and on track, something very important in IT project management. It also provided a process for conversation topics that fell outside the stated purpose to be addressed in subsequent conversations.

**Tips for Clarifying Purpose in Digital Communication:**

• **Start with a clear purpose statement:** At the beginning of every message, call, or meeting, clearly articulate what the conversation aims to achieve. For example, *"The goal of today's Zoom meeting is to finalize the marketing budget for Q1."* Endeavor to learn your team's nuances when communicating on various digital communication platforms.

• **Use structured agendas for meetings:** Digital meetings, especially video calls, can benefit from a clear agenda shared in advance. This ensures everyone knows what topics, aligned with the main purpose, will be covered so they can prepare accordingly.

• **Summarize the purpose frequently:** In longer digital conversations, regularly restate the purpose to keep the team focused. This is especially important in asynchronous communication, where participants may join a conversation at different times, often in the middle of the discussion. Restating the purpose maintains integrity, and keeps the context intact, leading to a more relevant digital conversation.

## Step Two: Call Out the Situation in Digital Communication

In digital environments, certain challenges of communication are unavoidable. Messages may be missed, time zone differences can cause delays, and some team members may struggle with the lack of face-to-face interaction. Leaders should proactively call out these challenges as relevant to the current state of digital communication and address them openly with respect to what an ideal state of digital communication should look like. Any gap between the two can be fleshed out before conversations go awry.

Acknowledging these barriers helps set realistic expectations and encourages team members to communicate more effectively within the limitations of the digital platforms.

Leaders must also address the different communication styles that emerge in digital environments. Some team members may feel comfortable using chat apps like Slack, while others may prefer emails or scheduled calls. By calling out these preferences and potential communication gaps, leaders can create more effective workflows and ensure that important messages are not lost in digital clutter.

**Example Situation:**

Ezra, the Sales Director, was managing a team that relied heavily on email for internal communication. He noticed that some of his newer team members, who were more accustomed to instant messaging apps like Slack, found it difficult to keep up with long email threads. To address this, during a team meeting Ezra surfaced the divergent current and preferred states between different digital communication approaches, called out the preferences shared by team members, and proposed a solution:

*"I know some of you prefer Slack and others are used to email. Let's establish clear guidelines for when we use each platform to ensure nothing gets lost during important conversations."*

This helped the team align their communication methods and openly share their preferences, particularly during times when it was important to maintain conversational integrity around current and future state dialogue. The shift led to increased respect among the team, reduced confusion within longer discussion threads, and created an environment that brought dispersed team members closer conversationally, while perhaps hundreds of miles apart physically.

**Tips for Calling Out the Situation in Digital Communication:**

• **Acknowledge the limitations of digital tools:** Address the challenges of digital communication head-on, such as time zone differences, message overload, or missed notifications. This sets realistic expectations for response times and reduces frustration.

• **Create communication guidelines:** Establish clear rules for when and how to use different digital tools. For example, Slack can be used for quick questions, while email is reserved for more formal, detailed communication. Discuss such rules with the team, so they are agreed upon as a unit rather than being simply handed down by the leader.

• **Encourage flexibility:** Not everyone will be equally as comfortable with every digital tool. Be open to using multiple platforms based on your team's preferences and needs. Give grace as team members, who are less experienced using a particular digital communication platform, learn it.

**Step Three: Consider Possibilities in Digital Communication**

Digital communication platforms, particularly video conferencing tools like Zoom and Google Meet, can sometimes feel impersonal or rigid. To foster engagement in virtual meetings, leaders must consider new possibilities for interaction, creativity, and collaboration. Video fatigue, a common issue in digital environments, can reduce productivity and morale if not managed effectively.

Leaders should actively explore ways to make virtual meetings more interactive and engaging, using digital communication platform features like breakout rooms, polling, or collaborative whiteboards. Since considering possibilities is often a meaty part of conversations, encouraging team members to participate actively - whether by leading discussions, presenting, or brainstorming – can help break up the monotony and keep everyone involved.

## Example Situation:

Molly, the VP of Lending, noticed that her team's weekly Zoom meetings were becoming less engaging, with most participants remaining silent while she led discussions around possibilities. She knew her team understood the digital communication platform they were using, so it felt clear that it was an engagement issue, not a technology issue.

To change this, Molly began rotating leadership roles based on the purpose of the conversation. Each week, a different team member would lead the conversation, probing and encouraging participation across the team to expand possibilities. Each team member was given autonomy to use platform features and tools as they saw fit to achieve their purpose. This resulted in an expansion of how the platform was used, incorporating interactive elements such as polls, and shared documents, interactive whiteboards, and of course greater live collaboration.

This shift led to more dynamic meetings, where everyone felt invested in the conversation and part of possibilities.

**Tips for Considering Possibilities in Digital Communication:**

• **Leverage interactive tools:** Use the features available in digital platforms to foster engagement, such as breakout rooms for small group discussions, polls to gather opinions, or shared documents for real-time collaboration and ideation.

• **Rotate leadership roles:** Encourage team members to take turns leading discussions, presenting options, or facilitating brainstorming conversations. This increases engagement and helps develop leadership skills at the same time.

• **Limit video fatigue:** Keep meetings short and focused. If possible, reduce the number of video meetings and consider alternatives like asynchronous updates through Slack or email. Consider human preferences that vary from team to team.

**Step Four: Calibrate Change in Digital Communication**

In digital environments, it is essential to have clarity around what will be measured and how results will be shared across the platform. Calibrating and communicating progress ensures measured activity is aligned with goals, and the team understands. In lieu of spontaneous check-ins and casual conversations that happen in an office setting, leaders must establish structured feedback loops and performance indicators. This ensures that team members stay on track and that leaders can adjust expectations or provide support where needed.

Digital tools offer various ways to measure performance and track progress, from project management software like Asana or Trello to team dashboards and task trackers.

Leaders should regularly check in with their teams, using these tools to review progress, identify obstacles, and adjust timelines as needed.

**Example Situation:**

Olivia, the Director of Information Technology, implemented a Trello board to manage her IT team's projects remotely. Each team member was responsible for updating their tasks regularly, allowing Olivia to track progress at a glance. She also scheduled weekly check-ins with each team member to review their progress and offer support. By calibrating progress through clear and transparent measures, Olivia was able to lead effective conversations by referencing updates shared openly on the digital application. This kept her remote team on track and allowed for re-calibration of ongoing deliverables to ensure project success.

**Tips for Calibrating Change in Digital Communication:**

• **Use project management tools:** Implement tools like Asana, Trello, or Monday.com to track tasks, deadlines, and progress in a centralized location. This provides for a common source of data, adding to conversation effectiveness and efficiency.

• **Establish regular check-ins:** Schedule one-on-one or team check-ins to review progress, discuss obstacles, and adjust timelines as needed. Calibration of how team members are feeling can be just as important as calibration of the activity expected to produce measured outcomes.

• **Focus on measurable outcomes:** In a digital environment, it is important to track clear, quantifiable metrics to ensure that the team is making progress toward its goals. Ask team members what digital mediums they prefer, as their comfort can decrease cycle time to get you the data you may need.

### Step Five: Commit To Act in Digital Communication

In a digital-first environment, committing to action involves not just setting goals but also optimizing workflows to ensure that communication and collaboration are efficient. This may involve refining the use of digital tools, streamlining processes, or introducing new software to address specific team needs.

Leaders must be proactive in identifying areas where digital workflows can be improved and commit to implementing changes that enhance productivity. This commitment should also extend to providing training and support to ensure that all team members are comfortable using the chosen tools. With digital competence comes a greater ability to maintain commitments. In the end, leaders must also remember that while digital communication platforms can be a source of efficiency, teams are made up of human beings. People-first is still most effective in solid leadership, and the digital tools used should be presented as supporting collective needs to foster effective conversations and overall communication.

### Example Situation:

Ezra, the Director of Sales, realized that his sales team was spending too much time coordinating tasks via email leading to inefficiencies, missed deadlines, and administrative waste during time sensitive conversations. After discussing this with his team, everyone committed to transitioning to a more streamlined digital workflow using Asana to manage tasks and deadlines. He provided training sessions to ensure that everyone was proficient with the new system and ensured everyone on the team felt both knowledgeable and able to utilize the platform and their new process successfully before rolling it out. Within a few weeks, the team saw a significant improvement in conversations that pulled on digital data, efficiencies in task management, clearer communication, and fewer delays.

**Tips for Committing to Act in Digital Communication:**

• **Identify bottlenecks:** Regularly review your team's digital workflows to identify areas where communication or cooperation is breaking down. Where those breakdowns adversely affect conversations, address them collaboratively.

• **Commit to the right tools:** Choose tools that address your team's specific needs and ensure that everyone is trained in how to use them effectively. Avoid making assumptions around levels of comfort using various digital tools and remember that knowledge and ability are different and distinct.

• **Be open to feedback:** Encourage your team to provide feedback on digital tools and workflows. Be willing to adjust based on their input, and shift where it makes sense for the team.

**CONCLUSION:**

**NAVIGATING DIGITAL COMMUNICATION PLATFORMS WITH THE ADAPTIVE CONVERSATION PROCESS**

Digital communication platforms offer powerful tools for connecting remote and hybrid teams, but they also require leaders to adapt their approach to conversation and collaboration.

The Adaptive Conversation Process provides a structured framework for managing these interactions, ensuring that digital conversations remain focused, purposeful, and engaging.

By using digital applications to capture and clarify purpose, calling out the situation using different digital communication approaches, considering possibilities through use of various digital features, calibrating change so it is both captured and transparent for adjustment where appropriate, and committing to act by blending optimized workflows and human connection, leaders can embrace digital communication platforms as a value-added way of ensuring effective and efficient conversations and realizing expected results.

## APPLYING THE ADAPTIVE CONVERSATION PROCESS TO NEGOTIATING CONVERSATIONS

Negotiation is a crucial skill in leadership and business, involving the delicate balance of advocating for one's own needs while understanding and considering the needs of others. Successful negotiations require clear communication, empathy, strategic thinking, and adaptability. Whether negotiating contracts, resolving conflicts, or establishing partnerships, leaders must navigate conversations that can be complex, emotional, and substantially outcome driven.

The Adaptive Conversation Process is highly effective in negotiations because it provides a structured yet flexible framework to ensure that each phase of the negotiation is approached with clarity, empathy, and a focus on finding mutually beneficial outcomes. The five steps: Clarify Purpose, Call Out the Situation, Consider Possibilities, Calibrate Change, and Commit to Act, all align well with the stages of a negotiation, helping leaders guide these types of conversations toward successful conclusions.

Likewise, leaders who utilize the Adaptive Conversation Process can have an easier time approaching negotiation from a "principled" perspective rather than a "positional" one, as suggested by authors Roger Fisher and William Ury in their book *Getting To Yes*. What we have learned from this is that principled negotiation is geared toward achieving outcomes that are clearly and mutually beneficial in achieving a positive end.

If we employ a principled approach in negotiation conversations, we focus on the interests of all parties and an objective standard to measure ideas against. In the Adaptive Conversation Process, this means clarifying that approach as part of the purpose up front, placing those interests on the table in terms of what is happening now compared to what ends each party is trying to achieve, and being prepared to engage in possibility-making together.

A principled approach helps broaden our vision in negotiation conversations and encourages us to invent several options while keeping an eye on mutual gains before making final decisions. In the Adaptive Conversation Process, this means dedicating ample time and energy to considering possibilities in a collaborative and respectful way as you explore options and roadblocks in an open and mutually supportive manner.

Finally, a principled approach guides us in separating the "people" from the "problem" or "situation" being negotiated. If we place whatever it is that we are negotiating or trying to solve in the center, openly between us, and look at it objectively and jointly, then our focus can rightfully be placed where it needs to be. Our conversation can feel like we are on the same team, collectively working to reach a decision point together rather than sitting on opposite sides of the table trying to push a single agenda or point of view. In the Adaptive Conversation Process, this means examining possibilities and agreed upon options and then calibrating actions and subsequent measurement in tandem. It encourages co-creation over command, and discussion over direction. It also makes it easier to wrap the conversation by gaining agreement on the next steps, as commitment has been negotiated together.

The Adaptive Conversation Process provides a structured framework for guiding negotiation conversations, ensuring that each step is approached in a thoughtful and intentional manner, increasing the odds of mutual success.

**Step One: Clarify Purpose in Negotiating Conversations**

Clarifying Purpose is critical in negotiations because it sets the foundation for the conversation. In any negotiation, both parties need to be clear on what they are trying to achieve. This includes understanding not only your own objectives but also the objectives of the other party. Clarifying purpose helps prevent misunderstandings and ensures that both sides are aligned to the goals of the negotiation.

In negotiations, clarifying purpose also involves setting the tone for the conversation. By starting the conversation with a clear understanding of what you hope to accomplish together, you can establish a collaborative, rather than adversarial dynamic. This helps create a principled environment where both parties are more likely to work toward a solution that benefits everyone.

**Example Situation:**

Molly, the VP of Lending, was negotiating a partnership agreement with a new fintech company. At the onset of the conversation, before engaging in substantial negotiation dialogue, Molly made a point to address the fintech's leadership team and say,

*"Our goal today is to create a partnership that enhances both of our offerings and meets the needs of our customers. There will certainly be ideas on how best to construct this partnership, and together we can construct a wise agreement. We want to ensure that this agreement benefits both sides and fosters a meaningful relationship."*

Everyone already knew what the meeting was for; however, by following the Adaptive Conversation Process and formally clarifying the purpose up front, Molly ensured everyone was on the same page and additionally set a cooperative tone for the negotiation, emphasizing principled mutual benefit over positional competitive negotiation.

### Tips for Clarifying Purpose in Negotiating Conversations:

• **State your objectives clearly:** Be transparent about what you want to achieve in the negotiation. This helps ensure the other party understands where you are coming from and what is important to you.

• **Acknowledge the other party's goals:** Recognize that the other party has objectives too and express your intent to find a solution that meets everyone's needs. Take time to ask about the other party's goals in the negotiation and be sure to include their objectives as part of the conversation's purpose.

• **Set a collaborative tone:** Emphasize that the goal of the negotiation is to reach a win-win outcome, rather than focusing solely on your own demands. Human beings can be competitive; however, they can be equally compassionate and caring. The tone you set in clarifying your purpose can bring out one more than the other.

### Step Two: Call Out the Situation in Negotiating Conversations

Clearly defining the current circumstances, needs, preferred end-game, and potential challenges in the negotiation are necessary early in the conversation. When describing the situation, both parties should articulate their perspectives, including any current, prior, or perceived future impediments that may be important to surface in the negotiation. Calling these elements out helps to ensure that both parties have a shared understanding of the context in which the negotiation is taking place.

In negotiations, calling out the situation also involves identifying potential sticking points or areas where disagreement may arise. By addressing these issues early in the conversation, you can prevent misunderstandings and be prepared proactively to find options once you have moved to the next step in the process. Calling out the situation requires active listening and empathy, as it is essential to understand the other party's position and concerns just as you understand your own.

**Example Situation:**

Ezra, the Director of Sales, was negotiating a contract renewal with a long-term client who had recently expressed concerns about pricing. During the negotiation, Ezra called out the situation by acknowledging the client's concerns:

*"I understand that certain internal and external conditions have you feeling pressure with respect to budget constraints, and that the current pricing model may not be sustainable for you. Let's discuss how we can address that while still providing the level of service you need."*

By calling out the situation, Ezra displayed that he was not preparing to negotiate for one-sided gain. He showed that he was attuned to the current reality his client was facing and that their needs would become part of the negotiation. By calling this out up front, Ezra was able to place an anticipated gap in the center – between them – so they could be prepared to discuss it collaboratively. Taking this step in their conversation helped to build trust and open the door to a constructive negotiation.

**Tips for Calling Out the Situation in Negotiating Conversations:**

• **Acknowledge concerns upfront:** Identify and call out potential issues or sticking points early in the conversation. This helps prevent surprises and shows that you are open to discussing the other party's concerns.

• **Use active listening:** Pay close attention to the other party's statements and body language to fully understand their position and concerns. This helps ensure something important does not get overlooked when calling out the situation, causing an inadvertent need to drift back to this step later.

• **Create a shared understanding:** Make sure both parties have a clear, shared understanding of the situation - current and desired state - including any constraints or challenges that may affect the negotiation.

**Step Three: Consider Possibilities in Negotiating Conversations**

Often, the bulk of a negotiation conversation includes exploring potential solutions and options. Both parties should engage in a collaborative process of brainstorming and considering different possibilities for reaching an agreement. This step is critical for fostering a sense of partnership and for finding creative solutions that can meet the needs of both sides.

In negotiation, it is important to approach this with an open mind, being willing to explore alternative solutions that you may not have initially considered. You can ask open-ended questions to encourage the other party to suggest options, while also offering your own ideas. This exploratory phase is crucial in the conversation for identifying win-win scenarios, where both parties feel they are gaining value in the negotiation.

**Example Situation:**

Carter, the Nursing Director, was negotiating a staffing contract with a healthcare provider. Both sides had different priorities. Carter needed more nurses on staff, but the provider had budgetary constraints. During the negotiation, Carter asked that they spend ample time considering possibilities that might meet both of their needs, encouraging the provider to engage in various brainstorming techniques.

They began with a mind-mapping exercise, followed by rapid ideation, before clouding ideas for a separate activity they might include nurses in to further expand possible options. They explored possibilities such as a phased staffing increase, where additional nurses would be hired gradually over six months, aligning with the provider's budget cycle. Their focus on openness to a wide range of options led to the right solution, fostering a sense of conversational collaboration and mutual benefit.

**Tips for Considering Possibilities in Negotiating Conversations:**

• **Encourage brainstorming:** Invite the other party to suggest options and alternatives. Use questions like, *"What other possibilities can we explore?"* or *"How might we structure this differently to meet both of our needs?"*

• **Be open to creative solutions:** Be willing to consider solutions that go beyond your initial position. Flexibility is key to finding win-win outcomes, and sometimes one possibility can spark an idea that leads to the best solution.

• **Focus on mutual benefit:** Look for opportunities to create value for everyone involved. Negotiations are most successful when the conversation leaves both parties feeling as though they have gained something meaningful from the agreement.


## Step Four: Calibrate Change in Negotiating Conversations

Setting and adjusting clear and actionable terms for the agreement, against which the successful solution or agreement will be measured, is a step too many people speed through. This is where the details of the negotiation are formalized, and both parties agree on specific terms and conditions.

In this phase it is important to be precise about deliverables by each party, which would indicate that expectations have been met. It is also a time for "if-then" discussion, as calibration includes indicating how both parties will know if actions have indeed met expectations, and what would adjust if certain events should occur.

In negotiating conversations, calibrating change means making sure that the final agreement is realistic and feasible for both parties before moving to commitment. This involves breaking down the agreement into specific actions or milestones and ensuring that both sides have a clear understanding of their responsibilities. This step also involves addressing any remaining concerns or ambiguities to prevent misunderstandings down the road.

## Example Situation:

Olivia, the Director of Information Technology, was negotiating a multi-year contract with a software vendor. After discussing various possibilities, they agreed on a customized pricing model that would allow Olivia's team to access additional features at a reduced rate. During the Calibrate Change phase in the Adaptive Conversation Process, Olivia and the vendor worked together to outline the specific terms of the agreement, including the pricing structure, software implementation timelines, and support services. They also added consideration for adjustments in utilization, which aligned to mutually agreed upon value. Data would be collected and shared over a twelve-month span, with calibration conversations to follow at quarterly intervals during the first year. By clearly defining these terms, both parties left the negotiation with a shared understanding of their respective responsibilities, and measured outcomes to track, analyze, and share.

## Tips for Calibrating Change in Negotiating Conversations:

• **Break down the agreement into clear terms:** Define the specific terms and conditions of the agreement, including timelines, deliverables, and any contingencies that might lead to a need for re-calibration.

• **Ensure both parties understand their responsibilities:** Clarify the roles and responsibilities of each party to ensure that the agreement is realistic and achievable. This is critical before moving toward commitment.

• **Address any ambiguities:** Take the time to address any remaining questions or concerns to prevent misunderstandings later in the process. Ensure measured outcomes are both calibrated and firmly understood, as anything left vague can create issues down the road.

## Step Five: Commit To Act in Negotiating Conversations

Commitment to act is the time in the conversation when both parties are ready to formalize their negotiated agreement and associated next steps. In this phase, the focus is on ensuring that both sides understand, are fully comfortable, and are ready to implement the agreed-upon terms. This step involves not only signing contracts or formal agreements but also establishing mechanisms for accountability and follow-up to ensure that the agreement is executed as planned.

In negotiation, committing to act also means maintaining a positive relationship with the other party after the agreement is reached. It is important to reinforce the collaborative spirit of negotiation and express a willingness to continue working together in the future. This helps build long-term trust and lays the groundwork for future negotiations.

## Example Situation:

Ezra, The Director of Sales, concluded a contract renewal negotiation with his client by finalizing the terms of the new agreement, which included adjusted pricing and additional support services. To ensure both parties were committed to the new terms, Ezra set up regular check-ins with the client to review their satisfaction with the service and address any potential issues. Likewise, his client promised to maintain transparency along the way, confirming a mutual dedication to trust. By committing to ongoing communication and support, their relationship was strengthened and set the tone for long-term success of the partnership.

## Tips for Committing to Act in Negotiating Conversations:

• **Formalize the agreement:** Ensure that both parties sign a formal contract or agreement that clearly outlines the terms. If it is important enough to be considered an expectation, then it should be included in writing to confirm a commitment to deliver.

• **Establish accountability mechanisms:** Set up regular check-ins or progress reviews to ensure that both parties are fulfilling their responsibilities. Remember, execution of that which was negotiated delivers a result, but commitment behind that execution builds trust.

• **Reinforce the relationship:** Express a commitment to maintaining a positive working relationship and continuing to collaborate in the future. Negotiations are between people, and in that regard, feelings will always be an important element in any negotiation conversation.

## CONCLUSION:

## APPLYING THE ADAPTIVE CONVERSATION PROCESS TO NEGOTIATING CONVERSATIONS

Negotiation is a complex process that requires strategic thinking, empathy, and adaptability.

The Adaptive Conversation Process provides structure so the conversation can progress intentionally along a path where mutual gain can be explored and validated along the way.

By clarifying purpose with a principled approach, calling out the situation so you understand the other party's position and concerns just as you understand your own, considering possibilities in a way that fosters a sense of partnership, calibrating change so both parties know if actions have met expectations, and committing to act by formalizing agreements and reinforcing collaboration, leaders can engage in effective negotiating conversations that achieve near-term results and build long-term relationships.

## APPLYING THE ADAPTIVE CONVERSATION PROCESS IN CUSTOMER SERVICE SITUATIONS

Customer service is the cornerstone of any successful business, but it can also be one of the most challenging areas to manage, especially when dealing with dissatisfied or difficult customers. Navigating these situations effectively requires empathy, patience, and a structured approach to resolving issues. Whether it is handling complaints, defusing tension, or addressing complex service failures, how leaders and customer service teams handle these conversations can make or break a company's reputation.

The Adaptive Conversation Process provides a practical framework for guiding customer service conversations. By using the five steps: Clarify Purpose, Call Out the Situation, Consider Possibilities, Calibrate Change, and Commit to Act, customer service professionals can approach difficult conversations with confidence, aiming to resolve issues in a way that enhances customer satisfaction and loyalty.

### Step One: Clarify Purpose in Customer Service Situations

In most customer service conversations, emotions tend to run high - for good or bad - which is why clarifying the purpose of the conversation is important. Just as you would in other types of conversations, actively listening first and then empathetically repeating back what you have heard as you clarify purpose is the best practice, and critical in customer service situations. Customers often contact service personnel when they are upset, frustrated, or confused, so it is essential to start the conversation by clarifying the purpose for the conversation to be had. Doing so helps set the table for a focused and constructive dialogue, while also assuring the customer that their concerns are being taken seriously.

In customer service situations, clarifying the purpose involves both listening to the customer's concerns and stating your intent to resolve the issue. By clearly explaining what the conversation aims to achieve, whether it is finding a solution, providing information, or escalating the issue, service representatives can help the customer feel heard and reassured from the start.

## Example Situation:

Olivia, Director of Information Technology, received a call one afternoon from an angry customer who was experiencing problems with their software. This customer somehow circumvented the general customer service line and made her way directly to Olivia's office phone. Rather than transferring the call, she decided to handle it herself. Olivia started the conversation by saying:

*"I understand you are having issues with the software, and I am here to help resolve that for you today. Let's use our time on this call to understand what is going on so we can work together in figuring out what may be causing the problem. Once we know, then I can work toward getting it fixed. Does that sound ok?"*

By first clarifying the purpose of the conversation, the caller fully understood exactly what would transpire on the call, which did not necessarily include an immediate solution. Olivia reassured the customer that her focus was on understanding, working together, and finding the right direction toward resolving the issue.

## Tips for Clarifying Purpose in Customer Service Situations:

• **Acknowledge the customer's issue:** Start by recognizing the customer's frustration or concern, showing empathy for their situation and ensuring they know you are listening.

• **State your intent clearly:** Let the customer know what the conversation is aiming to achieve such as gaining a full understanding, exploring possible solutions, or escalating the issue if necessary.

• **Set a positive tone:** Use calm, reassuring language to help the customer feel that they are in good hands and that their problem will be addressed.

## Step Two: Call Out the Situation in Customer Service Situations

Identifying and articulating the specific issue the customer is facing is an important step before advancing the conversation. A full understanding of what is happening compared to what should be happening must come before a solution. Often, customers struggle to explain the problem clearly, or they may focus more on their frustration than on the details of the issue. Your conversation should seek to draw out and clarify the situation. Asking the right questions and gathering the necessary information early in the conversation will help the conversation progress and avoid spinning.

Focus on understanding the issue and its root cause, if possible. By asking open-ended questions and summarizing the customer's concerns, you can help articulate and confirm the situation more clearly. This not only helps to diagnose the issue more effectively but also reassures the customer that they are being heard and understood.

### Example Situation:

Ezra, Director of Sales, was dealing with an important client who was upset about a delayed shipment. Ezra asked the client to describe what had happened:

*"Can you walk me through when you placed the order, what your delivery expectation was, and what communication you received about the shipping status?" It sounds like the shipment was delayed by the courier. I can see why that would be frustrating."*

By engaging in dialogue around both facts and expectations, Ezra ensured he understood the situation before discerning why something did not happen as planned. Clients want to feel as though you are on the same page as them before trying to solve their issue. Ezra asked important questions, showed that he was genuinely invested in hearing what was expected, and displayed empathy at this early stage in the conversation. By calling out the situation before moving too quickly, Ezra made the client feel better, even in a highly emotional state, an important first step in their conversation.

### Tips For Calling Out the Situation in Customer Service Situations:

• **Ask open-ended questions:** Encourage the customer to describe the problem in their own words. Customers want to tell you exactly what they have to say. Asking them to share helps ensure all aspects of the issue are conveyed and understood.

• **Summarize the issue:** Mirror what the customer said, and what their primary expectations are, to confirm that you fully understand the situation. This prevents the need to drift back once you have progressed in the conversation.

• **Show empathy:** Acknowledge the customer's frustration and express genuine empathy for their situation. This helps to defuse tension, build rapport, and open the conversation up in a healthy way.

### Step Three: Consider Possibilities in Customer Service Situations

Once it is time to consider possibilities, the conversation can begin to shift from understanding and diagnosing the issue to exploring potential alternatives or solutions. In customer service, this step is crucial for engaging the customer in the problem-solving process and offering them choices for how the situation can be resolved. Providing options gives the customer a sense of control and helps to turn a negative experience into a more positive one.

In customer service situations, it is important to be flexible and creative in considering solutions. This might involve offering refunds, exchanges, discounts, or other forms of compensation. The key is to find a solution that not only resolves the customer's issue but also leaves them feeling satisfied with the outcome. Considering possibilities in customer service also might include opportunities for service recovery, finding ways to move beyond making the customer whole and delivering something "extra" in the process. Adding service recovery to the conversation as part of considering possibilities can turn an angry customer into an appreciative one.

**Example Situation:**

Carter, the Nursing Director, was handling an escalated patient complaint about a billing error. After clarifying the situation and what was creating the patient's concern, Carter moved to considering possibilities:

*"What you are telling me is that the charge on your last bill was higher than you expected. Is that right? Sometimes the CPT code applied is different than you expect. CPT stands for "Current Procedural Terminology." These are codes associated with medical procedures and services. These codes inform your insurance, so they know what to cover. Would you rather contact your insurance company first to find out what code you expected, or would you rather I find out what code was used for the current billing?"*

Carter shared information that a patient may not already know, bringing them into the conversation at an even understanding. In offering possible choices, he empowered the customer to select a next step toward resolution that worked for them, increasing their satisfaction with the conversation and process.

**Tips for Considering Possibilities in Customer Service Situations:**

• **Offer multiple solutions:** Whenever possible, provide the customer with options for resolving the issue. This helps them feel more in control and increases satisfaction.

• **Be flexible:** Be open to considering creative or non-standard solutions that meet the customer's needs while maintaining company policies. The customer's idea of what is possible may or may not be feasible; however, listening at least engages them respectfully in the conversation toward a solution.

• **Focus on a positive outcome:** Frame possibilities in a way that emphasizes the benefits to the customer, helping to turn a negative experience into a positive one.

### STEP FOUR: CALIBRATE CHANGE IN CUSTOMER SERVICE SITUATIONS

Confirming how the issue will be resolved and how you will evaluate the degree to which that did the trick is an important final step in your conversation. In customer service, it is important to let the customer know that, while together you have agreed upon the best way to resolve their issue, you will not be satisfied until you have confirmed that their satisfaction has been achieved.

We are all human, so sometimes we choose the wrong next steps, and that is ok if the customer knows that you are making it your goal to follow up on things and shift if needed. This places you and the customer on the same side, helps manage their expectations, and ensures that both parties are aligned and committed to the solution.

### *Example Situation:*

Olivia, the Director of Information Technology, was handling an internal customer's software issue. The internal customer was a leader in the project management office, and the software challenge had the potential to set an important project back. Other dependencies in the project could also be adversely affected if the solution was not a quick fix.

In her conversation, Olivia and the PMO leader landed on two or three possibilities that could generate a rapid resolution, allowing the project and all dependencies to move forward, while long-term corrections in the software could be made. They spent time calibrating how the solutions would be measured with respect to achieving both near- and long-term goals, who would confirm success at each iterative sprint within the solution, and what adjustments would be made if any of the possibilities did not seem to be working as expected. By providing options and timely solutions, calibrating variables, and giving long-term assurances, Olivia ensured that her internal customer knew what to expect and felt comfortable going forward.

## Tips for Calibrating Change in Customer Service Situations:

• **Set time to calibrate:** Provide the customer with details on when certain actions will be initiated and discuss calibration. Then, ensure everyone knows when and how actions will be measured against solutions and outcomes.

• **Communicate your part:** Let the customer know what actions you will be taking and how you will be involved in making necessary adjustments if solutions are not achieving expectations against measured results.

• **Provide follow-ups:** If certain actions cannot be taken immediately, commit to regular updates on when they will be completed and what data you will return with to show decisions were appropriate and effective.

## Step Five: Commit To Act in Customer Service Situations

In customer service, it is important to tell the customer what they can expect next, provide a clear timeline for when they can expect it, and what actions (if any) they may need to take. This is crucial for building trust and ensuring that the customer feels that their issue has been fully addressed. In customer service, following through on your commitments is essential for maintaining customer loyalty and satisfaction.

Summarize the solution, confirm that the customer is satisfied with the resolution, and ensure that all actions will be completed in a timely manner. Remember, stating the next steps is not enough. Clear communication helps to build trust and shows the customer that their issue is being taken seriously. You must convey your commitment in a way that tells your customer they are important, and your time is well spent ensuring their satisfaction. If the issue requires further follow-up, clearly outline who will be responsible for that follow-up and when it will occur.

## Example Situation:

Ezra, the Director of Sales, engaged in an important customer service conversation with a large global client. The client's sales representative agreed to a six-month proof of concept at no cost, with a three-year contract to do business. There was some confusion around the timing of billing for the agreement, which Ezra immediately addressed:

*"I will contact our billing department today and ask them to push your invoice date out six months, into the new year. I know you have this investment set for next year's budget, and I apologize for the disconnect on our side. I will follow up internally to ensure this is complete and send you a*

*confirmation email once it is done. You will receive a corrected invoice within 30 days with the new due date. If there are questions on our side, I will handle them. You are my priority."*

By confirming the resolution and laying out the next steps clearly, Ezra showed the client that their concern would be taken care of. He also shared the steps he would personally take to show the client that they are important to him and the company. Commitment was on full display in this part of the conversation, beyond the mere steps he would take to achieve a resolution.

**Tips for Committing to Act in Customer Service Situations:**

• **Summarize the resolution:** Restate the solution that has been agreed upon and confirm that the customer is satisfied with the outcome. Be clear and make sure the customer feels your level of commitment.

• **Follow through on commitments:** There is nothing worse for a customer than being told something will be handled, only to find it has not. Ensure that all actions are taken in a timely manner and provide updates if necessary.

• **Maintain open communication:** Let the customer know that they can reach out for further assistance if needed and provide them with contact information for follow-up. If they feel that they are disconnected after the conversation, their heightened emotions will linger.

**CONCLUSION:**

## USING THE ADAPTIVE CONVERSATION PROCESS IN CUSTOMER SERVICE SITUATIONS

Customer service situations can be stressful and complex, especially when dealing with dissatisfied or upset customers.

Utilizing the Adaptive Conversation Process helps approach customer service in a structured and empathetic way. By having this structured conversational progression, you can devote critical energy to active listening, which is vital in customer service.

By clarifying purpose through intentional active listening and empathizing, calling out the situation to reassure the customer that they are being heard and understood, considering possibilities that give the customer a sense of control, calibrating change to share how you will evaluate the degree to which actions lead to solutions, and committing to act by sharing next steps and showing the customer that their issue is being taken seriously, you can navigating situations effectively to resolve issues and maintain relationships.

## APPLYING THE ADAPTIVE CONVERSATION PROCESS TO CONFLICT SITUATIONS

Conflict is an inevitable part of leadership, teamwork, and organizational dynamics. When handled well conflict can lead to growth, innovation, and stronger relationships; however, if mismanaged it can lead to resentment, reduced productivity, and long-term damage to working relationships. Whether it is a disagreement between colleagues, tension on a team, or a dispute with external stakeholders, leaders must be equipped to navigate these situations effectively.

The Adaptive Conversation Process offers a clear and structured framework for addressing conflict in a constructive, solution-focused manner. By following its steps, leaders can guide conflict conversations in a way that promotes understanding, resolves issues, and strengthens relationships.

### Step One: Clarify Purpose in Conflict Situations

In conflict situations, clarifying purpose is essential for establishing a partnered approach with a constructive rather than combative tone. Conflict often arises from misunderstandings, differing perspectives, or misaligned expectations. Clarifying the purpose of the conversation helps to shift the focus away from emotions and toward a clear goal of understanding the root cause of the conflict enroute to achieving a prosperous resolution.

At the start of a conflict conversation, state the purpose clearly to ensure that all parties understand that the goal is resolution, not blame or escalation. This helps create a space where participants feel safe to express their concerns, while also setting the expectation that the conversation will be solution oriented as opposed to pointing fingers or worsening feelings.

**Example Situation:**

Molly, the VP of Lending, was addressing a conflict between two team members, Michelle and Josh, who had been arguing over policy and variables while handling the approval and underwriting process for a key client. Molly began the conversation by clarifying the purpose:

*"We're here to listen to each other respectfully, and talk openly about the situation, as we work to find a resolution that benefits the client and our "one team" philosophy of work. The goal of this conversation is to understand each other's perspectives, be open to considering variables, and achieve consensus on a path forward."*

By clarifying the purpose up front, Molly set the stage for a constructive conversation focused on listening to each other as an important part of how they would talk through their conflicting perspectives. This relationship-focused element of purpose included a solution-focused expectation to reach a resolution, while expressing an equally as important expectation of doing so in a manner consistent with the team's culture. We must remember, especially in times when conflict threatens a team dynamic, that how we choose to interact is just as important as the solutions we arrive at. By clarifying purpose in this way, respectful agreement forward in the conversation was made possible.

**Tips for Clarifying Purpose in Conflict Situations:**

• **State the goal of resolution:** Clearly communicate that the purpose of the conversation is to resolve the conflict and find a way forward. Including how you will engage with each other is always appropriate, and aligning to culture or core values can help immensely.

• **Create a neutral tone:** Avoid language that assigns blame or escalates the tension. Use neutral language to set a calm, solution-focused tone. When people are in conflict, they instinctively mirror (at or above) the level of emotion put forward by others. As a leader, you can intentionally impact this level of emotional response.

• **Encourage openness:** Let all parties know that the conversation is an opportunity to express perspectives and work together. Conflict can be good or troublesome, depending on how you clarify openness among all parties up front.

### Step Two: Call Out the Situation in Conflict Situations

Allowing all viewpoints to be shared is something of a gatekeeper in identifying and articulating the specific issue. What one person sees can easily differ from what another person sees, which is why giving everyone a voice is at the heart of ensuring an effective conversation in a conflict situation. This step is critical because it ensures that all parties have a shared understanding of what is happening and what the conflict is about. Often, conflicts are fueled by misunderstandings or assumptions, so it is important to bring clarity to the situation by explicitly stating what the issue is and encouraging each party to share their perspective.

In this step of the Adaptive Conversation Process, the leader's role is to listen actively, ask clarifying questions, and help each party articulate what they are seeing, and their concerns, in a way that is constructive and respectful. Calling out the situation does not mean assigning blame;

rather, it is about making sure that everyone is on the same page and that the root of the conflict is understood. Only then can the conversation circle up on what everyone is seeking, and how to address any gaps that may exist based on different viewpoints.

## Example Situation:

Ezra, the Director of Sales, was addressing a conflict between two sales team members, Ryan and Tommy, who had been competing for the same prospect. Emotions escalated between the two in a weekly meeting, when both shared steps they took to engage with that company. After the meeting, Ezra sat down with them to have an open conversation and quell the tension between the two.

After clarifying the purpose for their conversation, He asked each of them to describe their perspectives and how they viewed the current situation. Ryan expressed frustration that Tommy had reached out to his client without consulting him first, while Tommy noted that the company was still a prospect as no current contract for service was in place. Clearly, there was a disconnect that served as a jumping off point for the conflict.

As it turned out, Ryan had previously worked with this client eighteen months prior. Tommy could not have been aware since he joined the team only fourteen months ago, and the CRM platform did not reflect an active contract. By calling out the situation and getting everything on the table from both perspectives, Ezra was able to surface the reality of how the misunderstanding began, refer to policy with respect to timing of assigned and unassigned prospects, and refocus the conversation on resolution. This also led the conversation down a beneficial path, as they prepared to generate possibilities on how the team might prevent similar issues in the future.

**Tips for Calling Out the Situation in Conflict Situations:**

• **Encourage sharing of perspectives:** Give each person an opportunity to explain their perspective on the situation. Try not to use the phrase, "side of the story" as it promotes a sense of opposition rather than partnership.

• **Focus on the issue, not the people:** Keep the conversation centered on the specific issue at hand, rather than personal attacks or character judgments. Making it personal can lead to heightened emotions, while focusing on the situation connects the conflicting parties to direct their combined energy at resolution, not at each other.

• **Ask clarifying questions:** If the situation is unclear or there are assumptions driving the conflict, ask questions to help bring clarity to the root cause. This helps tell the story between what each person is seeing versus seeking, while ensuring that all voices are heard.

**Step Three: Consider Possibilities in Conflict Situations**

Once the purpose is clear and an understanding of what is occurring within the conflict has been mutually shared, the conversation can shift from defining what is happening to exploring potential solutions. In this step of the Adaptive Conversation Process, the goal is to brainstorm options for resolving the conflict in a way that meets the needs of all parties and addresses the underlying issue. This step encourages creativity and collaboration, helping the parties move away from entrenched positions and toward a shared solution.

In conflict resolution, considering possibilities means exploring different ways to meet everyone's needs, looking for compromises, or identifying changes in behavior or processes that could prevent future conflicts. The leader should facilitate this discussion by asking open-ended questions and encouraging both parties to contribute ideas. Remember, exploring options also means calling out roadblocks that may have contributed to the conflict in the first place. This step in the Adaptive Conversation Process helps further join parties in ideating positive ways forward, in the wake of a challenging situation that made the conversation necessary in the first place.

## Example Situation:

Carter, the Nursing Director, was mediating a conflict between two nurses, Lexi and Brady, who had been clashing over shift responsibilities. The two had worked together for many years, but recent policy changes requiring new process formalities led to challenges around requirements for conflicting requests. When the two submitted for the same dates off from work, both for important family engagements, their emotions escalated quickly and led to the conflict.

After creating space for the situation to be called out, allowing both voices to be heard, emotions were brought down to a manageable level. Carter was then able to ask both to engage in a process of considering possibilities for resolving the scheduling issue, which included looking at the situation through a broader lens. They had previously only been looking at it from the perspective that one person had to lose for the other to win, while ignoring the possibility that a win-win solution might be possible if they looked to the larger team for help. Amber, another nurse on the team, had submitted for the same time off. Exploring solutions by including the team proved to be fruitful, as Amber's dates were flexible, and she was more than happy to adjust so that Lexi and Brady could attend their family functions. Additionally, by generating possibilities the team was able to discuss other ideas around rotating shifts, shared schedules, and communication channels that would make the new policy easier to navigate for everyone. By connecting on possibilities as opposed to colliding on positions everyone won, and harmony was restored.

### Tips for Considering Possibilities in Conflict Situations:

• **Encourage brainstorming:** Invite both parties to suggest potential solutions. Focusing on possibilities that move in a forward direction, rather than looking backward by rehashing the conflict, leads down a more positive path.

• **Look for compromises:** Help the parties jointly explore ways to meet in the middle. Making small adjustments that could satisfy both sides is sometimes much easier than the conflicting parties might think, if they only allow cooler heads to prevail.

• **Focus on the future:** Shift the conversation from the past (what went wrong) to the future (how to prevent similar issues from arising). Conflict resolution includes finding answers in the moment, as well as avoiding challenges in the future.

### Step Four: Calibrate Change in Conflict Situations

Calibrating change involves turning possibilities that have been generated into specific, actionable, and (importantly) measurable agreements, and dedicating energy in the conversation to pressure-test how you will be able to tell if they are meeting resolution expectations. In conflict situations, it is important that both parties leave the conversation with a clear understanding of what will change or occur, what behaviors or actions are expected moving forward, and how all of this affects the situation in terms of a positive resolution. Calibrating change ensures that actions to be taken are laid out in a manner that communicates clear reasoning behind them in how they achieve an amicable outcome.

During this phase, the leader should work with both parties to clarify and discuss how the steps they will take will achieve the agreed-upon solution. It is important that this be a two-way sincere acknowledgement, otherwise actions taken by one party or the other risk being completed without full resolution of the conflict interpersonally. This might involve changes in communication, behavior, or processes. The leader should also establish benchmarks or checkpoints to review progress and ensure that actions do indeed meet expectations for conflict resolution.

**Example Situation:**

Olivia, the Director of Information Technology, was mediating a conflict between two team members who had been struggling to collaborate effectively on a project for a new mobile application. The two teammates agreed upon what the application should look like in its end-state; however, they had differing opinions on the order in which certain phases of the project should take place.

After discussing the situation in a respectful and open manner, and exploring possible steps that made sense to both, they agreed to find a new project management tool that broke down real and perceived dependencies in a more contextual manner. Engaging intentionally in this step of the Adaptive Conversation Process ensured they discussed to what degree they would know if that would help solve their conflict.

They agreed to work together on researching options and beta test any new application prior to full implementation. Olivia helped further calibrate change by remaining engaged as they researched options. At one point, Olivia found that working only among themselves was not meeting the expected change in a timely manner, so additional calibration led to including someone from the project management office. Through regular check-ins, calibrated adjustments, and ultimately a new application, not only was the conflict resolved but the entire team benefitted in better transparency across project dependencies and increased communication overall.

**Tips for Calibrating Change in Conflict Situations:**

• **Set specific and measurable agreements:** Work with both parties to outline the specific actions they will take to resolve the conflict. Then, dedicate time to discuss how you will measure whether those steps are meeting a mutual plan toward resolution.

• **Establish clear expectations:** Make sure that both parties understand their roles and responsibilities in taking actions. Likewise, flesh out who will be responsible for measuring and sharing data, keeping in mind that any calibration to actions would be made collectively.

• **Create accountability:** Set up regular check-ins or follow-up meetings to ensure that the steps toward a solution are working. The conflict will only be fully resolved when calibrated changes are confirmed and disagreeing parties have found harmony.

## Step Five: Commit To Act in Conflict Situations

When both parties to a conflict agree upon changes and take ownership of their roles in ensuring actions will meet mutual expectations toward resolving the conflict, the conversation can move to finalizing commitments. This closing step in the Adaptive Conversation Process is crucial for ensuring that the conversation leads to lasting change. In conflict situations, it is important for both parties to leave the conversation with a sense of responsibility for what will happen next, as well as for making the relationship or process work more smoothly going forward.

The leader's role in this phase is to ensure final clarity of the next steps among all who are involved, and to also reinforce ownership of guarantees made during the conversation. Both parties must feel trusted, comfortable, and supported in following through on their actions. This might involve providing additional resources, connecting with other stakeholders, scheduling follow-up meetings, or offering other ongoing support to help both parties navigate any challenges that arise as they implement the agreed-upon solutions.

## Example Situation:

Ezra, Director of Sales, concluded a conflict resolution conversation between two sales representatives, Gregory and Rachel. As a newer member of the team, Gregory was assigned a mentor in Rachel. As for Rachel, serving as a mentor was something of a stretch assignment to help her grow on the path to sales management. Their interactions started worsening after a few months, as Gregory had prior sales experience and wanted to move faster than Rachel was comfortable with in her new role as mentor. After a lengthy and very mutually beneficial conversation, Ezra confirmed commitments to specific actions from both. Gregory agreed to keep Rachel better informed about his prospecting activities and upcoming meetings to respect her growth toward leadership. Rachel committed to respecting Gregory's prior experience in sales by requiring less while inquiring more with respect to how she might best support him in gaining traction in his new environment. Beyond the agreement alone, Gregory and Rachel committed genuinely to one another's success.

Ezra scheduled a follow-up meeting three weeks after their initial conversation to review how the approach was working and to address any remaining concerns. By formalizing these commitments, Ezra ensured that both parties understood their commitments to one another, felt accountable for their part in the resolution, and were dedicated to maintaining a positive working relationship.

**Tips for Committing to Act in Conflict Situations:**

• **Verbalize commitment:** Summarize the agreements made during the conversation and ensure that both parties are committed to following through on the actions discussed. Commitment in conflict conversations is, in some ways, even more important than the actions alone.

• **Reinforce accountability:** Establish mechanisms for accountability, such as regular check-ins or progress reviews. These ensure both parties are following through, and that commitments are still felt earnestly.

• **Provide ongoing support:** Offer additional resources or support to help both parties implement the agreed-upon changes. Conflict resolution is a process and maintaining a connection from the first conversation through resolution and beyond helps maintain positive relationships.

## CONCLUSION:

## USING THE ADAPTIVE CONVERSATION PROCESS IN CONFLICT SITUATIONS

Conflict, when handled constructively, can lead to stronger relationships, improved processes, and greater understanding within teams.

The Adaptive Conversation Process is an important tool offering established points of reference, as emotions can quickly take things off-track. As a structure for the conversation, this is a step-by-step progression to help keep the train on its tracks.

By clarifying purpose to create space for a solution-oriented conversation, calling out the situation to give everyone a voice, considering possibilities that move away from entrenched positions and toward a shared solution, calibrating change to pressure-test if actions are meeting expectations, and committing to act by fostering a sense of responsibility and ownership, you can help resolve conflict in a way that maintains relationships. By using this framework in conflict situations, leaders can guide conversations in a way that promotes openness, fosters collaboration, and leads to lasting resolutions.

# 4.4

# Practice & Skill Development

## PART OF A PRACTICAL TOOLSET

The Adaptive Conversation Process is not just a theoretical framework, but part of a practical toolset that leaders, coaches, mentors, consultants, and trainers can apply to many types of real-world conversations. Like with any process, the most important thing to do is:

Practice...Practice...Practice.

Developing proficiency using the Adaptive Conversation Process requires a commitment to repetition, self-awareness, and a dedication to ongoing learning.

By utilizing this as a critical tool for effective conversations, and by blending its use with the development of skills that go together with effective communication, leaders can create conversations that are highly effective in achieving desired outcomes.

The combination of structured communication, active engagement, and measurable actions leads to better results and stronger, more focused relationships across all levels of leadership and team dynamics.

## LEADERSHIP DEVELOPMENT

One of the most valuable aspects of the Adaptive Conversation Process is its real-world application and the tangible results it delivers, especially for leadership development. Over the years, we have had numerous opportunities to introduce the Adaptive Conversation Process to leaders across industries, and the impact has been both measurable and transformative.

Every leader has a widely diverse number of "at bats" to practice using the process across the many types of conversations it can adapt to. For this reason, we have found that leaders often benefit from a focused approach to developing proficiency using it with one kind of conversation first. Getting comfortable and proficient with it for a specific type of conversation makes it much easier to adapt it to other types of conversations. Everyone learns at a different pace, and leaders expand their learning and proficiency differently. Over time, the process itself becomes second nature, and the value of adaptability becomes clear in a very tangible way.

For instance, one group of leaders we worked with focused on using the Adaptive Conversation Process to structure their coaching conversations in a way that made them more focused, productive, and impactful. This led to better alignment between leaders and their teams, improved team performance, and a noticeable shift in the organization's coaching culture. Once leaders felt comfortable using the Adaptive Conversation Process in coaching conversations, they felt ready to begin using it intentionally in difficult performance conversations as well.

Trying to do anything all at once can make learning any new skill, tool, or process feel like a large mountain to climb. By focusing on learning to use the Adaptive Conversation Process for the type of conversation that makes most sense for you, in a way that aligns with personal, professional, or organizational goals, you give yourself an opportunity to practice and be successful with it in a narrow context before putting a heavier burden on yourself to be proficient in a broader one.

## ROME WASN'T BUILD IN A DAY

As with learning any new tool, skill, or process, it is important to give yourself grace, and the gift of time.

Do you recall earlier in this book when we shared the story of an organization that we worked with who told us it was better to tell someone, *"It is my pleasure"* than to say, *"No problem,"* a much more common response? Remember how awkward we said it felt to be saying *"my pleasure"* every time we delivered a service, or opened a door for someone, or picked up someone's keys after they dropped them for that matter? It felt strange but we forced ourselves to push through the awkward feelings. We set aside how clunky it felt at first and were steadfast in using this new phrase...until it felt normal and became second nature. It is the same here, as you learn to use the Adaptive Conversation Process.

Giving yourself grace means forgiving yourself when you try something and make a mistake. Be understanding, kind to yourself, and persevere. Conversations are complex interactions and learning a new process, especially one that presents such a fantastic opportunity for effectiveness can take time. Give yourself that gift. Invest in yourself by practicing, being good with progress over perfection, and celebrating as you get better and better.

When you first put the Adaptive Conversation Process into practice, it is likely that you will be making a change, or at least being more intentional, compared to how you have historically approached conversations. Do not give up, even if it feels forced or awkward at first, and give yourself grace to learn and adjust as you go.

We have even found that it can be helpful to share with the person you are having a conversation with (up front) that you are practicing a new conversation process as part of your own development, and that you appreciate their grace as you take your time or even pause to look down at your notes. This kind of authenticity and transparency humanizes even the most senior leaders and can have a positive impact on your conversations.

## DEVELOPING PARALLEL SKILLS

Think of "parallel skills" as secondary skills that run alongside a primary skill being developed or accessed. Those secondary skills simultaneously aid in successfully executing the primary skill. For instance, learning a new dance is made easier when parallel skills of rhythm, balance, and expression are simultaneously engaged. Becoming a skilled driver is improved when parallel skills of body control, observation, and anticipation are simultaneously engaged. When learning something new, one skill can often augment or complement the development of another skill. It is for this reason that leaders should actively develop and tap into parallel skills that improve communication, as these help in gaining proficiency using the Adaptive Conversation Process. We have included a few relevant parallel skills and techniques below.

## ACTIVE LISTENING

One of the cornerstones of effective communication is active listening. This skill is critical throughout all stages of the Adaptive Conversation Process, especially during steps like **Clarifying Purpose** and **Calling Out the Situation**. To develop this skill, consider practicing the following techniques:

- **Mirroring**: Repeat or paraphrase what the other person has said to ensure mutual understanding. This reinforces clarity and encourages deeper engagement.

- **Non-Verbal Cues**: Pay attention to body language, eye contact, and facial expressions, as these can indicate how the other person feels about the conversation and help you adjust accordingly.

- **Summarizing**: At key points in the conversation, provide a summary to confirm alignment and prevent misunderstandings. This technique helps in keeping the conversation focused and clear.

## FRAMING CONVERSATIONS

Framing is a powerful skill for setting the stage for productive dialogue. In the Clarify Purpose step for instance, framing helps define the scope and goals of the conversation. When done effectively, it provides a reference point to return to if the conversation drifts.

- **Big Picture Framing:** Before diving into details, offer a broad overview of the conversation's purpose, so everyone understands its importance. Sometimes discussing the high-level can help with mutual understanding once you get into the detail.

- **Contextual Framing:** Relate the conversation to broader business or personal objectives to demonstrate relevance and urgency. Relevance and relatability are key to connectedness in almost any conversation.

**OPEN-ENDED QUESTIONING**

Being skilled at asking open-ended questions is essential, especially for example during the Consider Possibilities and Calibrate Change steps. These types of questions encourage dialogue, exploration, and engagement, helping uncover new perspectives and deeper insights.

- **"What if..." Questions:** Pose hypothetical questions to explore new possibilities and break away from fixed thinking.

- **"How might we..." Questions:** This phrasing invites collaboration and creative problem-solving by focusing on collective action and innovation.

- **"Can You Tell Me More..." Questions:** Encourage further explanation or clarification on a particular point, ensuring thorough understanding before moving forward.

**SMART GOAL SETTING**

Particularly during the Commit to Act step, SMART goals (Specific, Measurable, Achievable, Relevant, and Time-bound), introduced by George T. Dorian in 1981, are instrumental in turning conversations into actionable plans. Leaders and teams should practice creating SMART goals and work together to define:

- Specific goals that outline exactly what needs to be accomplished.

- Measurable outcomes that allow progress to be tracked and evaluated.

- Time-bound commitments that establish clear deadlines for actions.

By using SMART goal setting, participants are more likely to commit to the actions outlined during the conversation and take ownership of the results.

## FEEDBACK

Being skilled at giving and receiving feedback is important, especially for leaders.

To reinforce continuous improvement and development, create feedback sessions or outlets that allow for regular follow-ups and adjustments. This is particularly useful in the Calibrate Change and Commit to Act steps.

- **Regular Check-Ins:** Schedule periodic reviews to assess progress on agreed actions. This ensures accountability and keeps the momentum going.

- **Iterative Improvement:** Based on feedback, fine-tune the approach as necessary, ensuring that learning and adjustments are an ongoing part of the process.

## ROLE-PLAYING

To help develop skilled use of the Adaptive Conversation Process, practice through role-playing or simulation exercises. These controlled environments allow individuals to refine their use of the steps in various scenarios such as coaching, mentoring, or performance-related conversations.

- **Peer-to-Peer Role-Playing:** Engage in role-playing sessions with colleagues or team members to practice the different stages of the Adaptive Conversation Process using real-life situations.

- **Scenario-Based Training:** Develop case studies and scenarios that mimic actual challenges you and other leaders are experiencing, allowing participants to work through them using the Adaptive Conversation Process.

## MEASUREMENT

Seeing patterns and effective measurement is an important skill. To ensure that the Adaptive Conversation Process is effectively applied, measure outcomes with clear, quantitative or qualitative metrics. During the Calibrate Change step, define how you will gauge and measure success.

- **Performance Measures:** These could include improvements in key performance indicators (KPIs) like sales, project completion rates, or customer satisfaction.

- **Behavioral Measures:** These track changes in team dynamics, leadership development, or employee engagement following key conversations.

By regularly measuring outcomes and providing feedback, leaders can refine the application of the Adaptive Conversation Process and ensure continuous improvement.

# SELF-REFLECTION AND CONTINUOUS LEARNING

After each conversation where you apply the Adaptive Conversation Process, tap into self-reflection skills and techniques to understand what worked and where improvements can be made. This reflective practice helps in developing proficiency with the framework over time.

- **Journaling:** After key conversations, jot down observations, lessons learned, and areas for improvement.

- **Feedback from Peers or Coaches:** Request feedback from those you have engaged with in conversations to get an external perspective on your communication effectiveness.


# LEVERAGING TECHNOLOGY FOR ACCOUNTABILITY

Being skilled using tools like project management software, collaborative platforms, or performance tracking systems can assist in maintaining accountability during the Commit to Act phase. Integrate technology to streamline follow-ups and track progress on agreed-upon actions.

- **Task Management Systems:** Use platforms like Trello, Asana, or Monday.com to document action items and ensure visibility and accountability.

- **Collaboration Tools:** Leverage tools like Slack or Microsoft Teams to keep conversations and follow-ups organized.

# Appendix
# Early Results

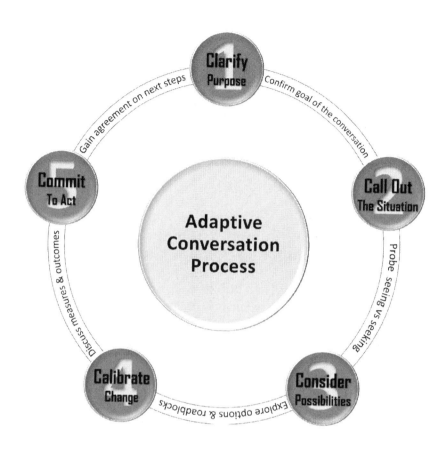

## SEEING RESULTS

Across executive leadership and consulting, we have had the privilege of leading transformative initiatives across industries, applying key leadership and diversity, equity, and inclusion (DEI) strategies, and guiding meaningful conversations of all kinds.

Over the course of our seasoned careers including executive roles, committee and board memberships, entrepreneurial endeavors, speaking engagements, and more we have seen firsthand how important structured, adaptive conversations can be in fostering meaningful change. This aligns seamlessly with the Adaptive Conversation Process, which we have used in many instances to guide leadership teams, improve communication, and drive organizational success. Here, we would like to share a few summarized examples that highlight how the Adaptive Conversation Process has played a pivotal role in our work and has garnered tangible results.

## EXAMPLE #1

### Clarifying Purpose – Integrating DEI at an Academy Award winning computer animation film studio

At this computer animation film studio, we worked on building leadership capabilities through a DEI lens, and the first step in every conversation was clarifying purpose. The studio had a creative culture deeply rooted in collaboration, but their leadership recognized the need to intentionally include diverse perspectives in their decision-making processes. During sessions with their senior leadership, the conversation often began with clarifying the objective for that conversation, not jumping ahead by suggesting or adding DEI initiatives for compliance. This ensured up front an objective to embed inclusion into the very DNA of their creative process.

This clarity of purpose allowed the studio to focus not only on increasing diversity but also on ensuring those diverse voices had an impact on how stories were told, characters were developed, and audiences were engaged. This aligns with the Adaptive Conversation Process' principle of clarifying why a conversation or initiative is happening in the first place, making it easier to align all stakeholders toward a common goal.

# EXAMPLE #2

## Calling Out the Situation – Identifying Barriers at a Top Ten Bank *(by Asset size)*

When we worked with this bank on leadership and workforce engagement, their senior leaders were trying to bridge the gap between internal workforce management and recruiting goals and expected strategic results. Through several coaching sessions, we consistently called out the situation being addressed to put what was occurring on the table. This allowed us to align it with what ideal expectations were, and to effectively address the disconnect between leadership intentions and client perceptions.

For example, some team members viewed the expanded recruiting processes, efforts, and activities that were put in place at the time as merely checkbox exercises rather than something that would help achieve core business strategies. By recognizing and openly discussing this perception gap early in our conversation we were able to surface deeper issues later, such as lack of communication, inconsistent training, and disconnected accountability. This aligns with the Adaptive Conversation Process' principle of calling out what leadership was seeing versus what they were seeking or sought to achieve. Openly identifying and verbalizing the current reality, even though it was uncomfortable, allowed the bank's leadership team to address it collaboratively head-on and meet all measures of success.

# EXAMPLE #3

## Considering Possibilities – Leadership Development at a Global Leader in Climate and Sustainability

At this organization, we spent a significant amount of time in every conversation considering possibilities that encouraged leadership to think outside the box when building inclusive teams. Initially, the leaders were focused on standard DEI training modules, but through a series of facilitated conversations, we explored other possibilities, such as integrating DEI into performance metrics and succession planning.

By considering these possibilities, the organization's leadership moved from passive DEI practices to active, measurable initiatives. They began to focus on cultivating an inclusive environment that encouraged innovation, rather than simply meeting diversity targets. Committing vast amounts of energy in this way aligns with the Adaptive Conversation Process' principle of considering possibilities. Even in the face of initial opposition or stalled initiatives, engaging in this step helped surface obstacles and exponentially ideate around new approaches. Leaders were encouraged to imagine what was possible and empowered to take bold actions, which led to tangible growth.

## EXAMPLE #4

### Calibrating Change – Measuring Impact at a National Latino Professional Association

Within the executive leadership office at one of the nation's leading Latino professional organizations, we led initiatives focused on executive learning and development. During these initiatives, we often found that measuring success was a challenge. That is where calibrating change became crucial. It was easy to coordinate around what we might build or what actions might be taken; however, once we intentionally took time in conversations to calibrate, assess, and adjust actions we saw real progress. In one of our programs, with one of the largest global leaders in the retail space, we invested significant energy in calibrating change during conversations. This established the opportunity to dialogue around metrics, and led to adjustments in how specific leadership development efforts were improving representation and inclusion at senior levels.

By setting specific and measurable outcomes such as increasing Latino representation in leadership by 10% within two years, and spending time calibrating up front and along the way to what degree actions were achieving expectations, the association helped that retailer create accountability and long-term sustainability for their goals.

## EXAMPLE #5

### Commit to Act – Driving Leadership Diversity in Healthcare

Engaged in a meaningful consulting relationship, we worked extensively with a large healthcare organization to improve leadership skills. The organization was undergoing a significant transformation, with a focus on improving leadership effectiveness in coaching conversations, strategic planning discussions, and performance management reviews. We introduced the Adaptive Conversation Process as part of this broader leadership development initiative. During our conversations with their executive team, we paused intentionally and fully to draw out commitments to act before moving to close out regular and intermittent meetings. We made extensive headway agreeing on concrete, measurable actions that were timebound with respect to when each type of conversation would become the focus for development. At every turn we collectively agreed to validate commitment as a core value in our conversations.

The healthcare organization committed to engaging with us long-term to design, develop, and deploy leadership development programming that phased in each of their three focus areas, ensuring the constant across all was the Adaptive Conversation Process. A commitment to integrate the process into leadership development programs and to promote its use with first and second level leaders to begin with was foundational. All actionable steps were not just discussed; they were clearly documented, assigned to accountable champions, and incorporated into their transformation plans.

Within six months, leaders who used the Adaptive Conversation Process saw a 40% improvement in their leadership effectiveness scores, as measured by employee surveys and 360-degree feedback. The following year, employee engagement surveys showed a 35% increase in engagement levels, with many employees attributing the change to the commitment of leaders and the improved quality of conversations they were having with them.

This success reinforced the importance of committing to act, as that commitment turned functional implementations into transformational and measurable outcomes that meant something special at the organization's core. Through collective commitment, holding each other accountable, and tracking progress we ensured that conversations did not stop at the planning stage but led to real, sustainable change.

## EXAMPLE #6

### The Adaptive Conversation Process: A Solution in Improving Coaching at Two Different Financial Institutions

Working directly with varied levels of leadership, we have had the pleasure of implementing the Adaptive Conversation Process to improve coaching. At one organization, we focused on sales leadership, and at the other organization we focused on the entire leadership population.

Both financial organizations were among leaders in their space (by asset size) and had similar levels of development when it came to coaching. Both had some level of leadership development over the years, yet neither had a centralized or consistent process for leaders to follow when it came to coaching conversations.

In collaboration with the executive team, the learning and development department, and human resources we structured an approach to introduce the Adaptive Conversation Process to organizational leaders. We began with initial communication with leaders so they would understand what we would be introducing, and why, and followed up with group training. We measured a baseline up front through surveying the direct reports of the leaders we were teaching to use the Adaptive Conversation Process and followed up with the exact same survey three to four months later.

In both financial organizations, across sales leaders in one and the full leader population in the other, we achieved nearly identical results:

**Financial Institution #1 - Sales Leaders:**

51% increase in **quantity** of coaching

61% increase in **quality** of coaching

------------------------------------------------------------------------

**Financial Institution #2 – All Organizational Leaders:**

50% increase in **quantity** of coaching

60% increase in **quality** of coaching

What truly amazed us is that in both financial institutions there was support from the top for the initiative, yet there was no specific requirement placed upon leaders. They were not assessed on their performance with coaching, nor was there any consequence for lack thereof. This was intentional, as we did not want our results to be skewed by stern executive expectations or motivated by anything more than how the Adaptive Conversation Process could help them be better coaches for their teams.

As a side note, we followed the same implementation with leaders at another organization with respect to having difficult performance conversations. While that organization did not want to engage in formal measurement, anecdotal qualitative results indicated similar success among people-leaders and their conversations.

## SUMMARY OF EARLY RESULTS FROM IMPLEMENTATION OF THE ADAPTIVE CONVERSATION PROCESS

Across various organizations and industries, the Adaptive Conversation Process has consistently proven to be a powerful tool for enhancing leadership communication and effectiveness.

Whether applied in coaching, mentoring, performance, teaching, training, consulting, advising, change, or other strategic discussions, it drives results by:

• **Increasing the frequency and quality of critical conversations:** Leaders become more proactive in engaging with their teams, and more deliberate and effective in how they approach each conversation.

• **Improving leadership effectiveness:** The structured approach of the Adaptive Conversation Process helps leaders align their teams around clear goals and outcomes, leading to measurable improvements in leadership effectiveness.

• **Driving organizational change:** In environments undergoing transformation, the Adaptive Conversation Process facilitates clearer communication, helps resolve conflicts, and fosters a culture of accountability and collaboration.

These results highlight the practicality and versatility of the Adaptive Conversation Process, making it an extremely valuable tool for leaders looking to improve their communication skills and drive positive outcomes within their organizations.

## CONCLUSION

We cannot say this often enough: The Adaptive Conversation Process is more than just a theoretical framework. It is a practical tool that we have applied to achieve transformational results. Whether working with Fortune 500 companies, small to mid-sized businesses, or advising non-profit organizations, the Adaptive Conversation Process has proven to be a reliable framework for structured, impactful conversations.

By clarifying purpose, calling out the situation, considering possibilities, calibrating change, and committing to act, we have led incredibly successful conversations and helped organizations not only meet but exceed their goals. The real-world examples we shared showcase how the Adaptive Conversation Process can drive meaningful change, both in leadership teams and in broader organizational culture.

The value of The Adaptive Conversation Process is that it provides leaders with a complete and powerful conversational progression to be effective.

The simplicity of the Adaptive Conversation Process is that its five linear steps provide an ideal progression, generating effectiveness and efficiency, so leaders spend less time and effort moving from one model to another, and focus their energy being fully present in the conversation at hand.

The inclusiveness of the Adaptive Conversation Process is that it does not require that you forego your pre-existing philosophical frameworks. Leaders who resonate with certain approaches or popular models can still honor them while integrating their tenets into dialogue as they follow the Adaptive Conversation Process.

The power of the Adaptive Conversation Process is that it is flexible and applicable to so many different types of conversations leaders have. Its greatest strength is in its name - that it is "adaptive" - meaning it can be used effectively for different types of conversations.

In an ever-changing world, there is a clear sense of urgency around the effectiveness of conversations, one of the most critical skills a leader can have. We have found the Adaptive Conversation Process to be consistent and impactful at every turn. Let it be the most important, single "adaptive" conversation process in your toolbox, and start engaging people in the most effective conversations you've ever led.

# About The Authors

# Nicholas Phillips, M.Ed, ACC, CCP, CPM

Nicholas is a seasoned learning, leadership, and organizational development professional, with measured success engaging collaboratively with employees and clients at all levels.

Breaking into the L&D field in 1999, he collaborated to build a corporate university that found its place on Training Magazine's very first *"Top 50 Learning Organizations"* list. Partnering through authentic university and fraternity relationships, he led training and corporate communications in the construction industry before joining a boutique HR consulting firm where he executed diverse talent and organizational development initiatives, engaging with companies from 3 to 30,000 employees globally.

Nicholas' corporate roles have included leadership from the front-line to the executive level, across industries such as global banking & finance, healthcare, manufacturing, and more. He has spearheaded top-level business initiatives, transformed the culture of leadership, built capacity and effectiveness, standardized internally and externally facing conversational effectiveness, built competency models, created emerging leader and succession programs, and led learning-focused high performance cultural transformations.

He holds a Master of Education in adult learning and development, global credentials in coaching and change management, and certifications in several competency assessments including emotional intelligence and more. Over the years, he has served as a speaker at conferences and leadership summits and is a thought-leader in talent development, enterprise learning, organizational interventions and strategy, leadership development, and conversational effectiveness.

# Suri Surinder

Suri Surinder is a seasoned executive with over 30 years of experience spanning leadership, diversity, equity, and inclusion (DEI) initiatives across various sectors.

He is the co-founder and CEO of CTR Factor, a woman-owned, minority-owned advisory services firm specializing in leadership and DEI consulting. Under his leadership, CTR Factor has served hundreds of companies across dozens of different industries, including notable clients such as PwC, RSM, Crowe Horwath, Prudential, Pixar, Ingersoll Rand, PNC, & AICPA.

Throughout his career, Surinder has held significant roles in the C-Suite leading multi-billion-dollar regions and spearheading global business transformations. His experience spans decades as an executive, consultant, board member, author, entrepreneur, and professor.

In addition to his executive roles, Surinder is a prolific writer and speaker on topics related to leadership and workplace culture. His insights have garnered significant attention, with social-professional engagement amassing over 1.5 million global views across a following of more than 51,000 connections.

Suri is also the author of *The Hidden Science of CTR Factor Leadership: Book 1 - The Three Basic Questions*, which delves into the scientific principles of effective leadership.

He has a BS in Civil Engineering, MS in Structural Engineering, MBA in Marketing, and a DBA in Strategy.

We hope that this book, and the Adaptive Conversation Process, has inspired you just as it has inspired us and so many other leaders with whom we have already shared this.

You are probably eager to put this book down and schedule your next coaching or mentoring session, difficult performance conversation, or any number of others you may already have on your calendar.

In addition to this book, the workshop we bring to companies teaches leaders how to have effective conversations using this process – whether coaching, mentoring, performance, consulting, advising, teaching, training, change, etc.

For information regarding speaking engagements or for programming to bring the Adaptive Conversation Process to your company, contact Nicholas Phillips and Suri Surinder at:

Email: info@CTRfactor.com

Web: CTRfactor.com

Phone: 1 (877) 275-9472

Made in the USA
Columbia, SC
29 June 2025

59960697R00170